The Hampstead Book
The A-Z of its history and people

First published 2009
by Historical Publications Ltd
32 Ellington Street, London N7 8PL
(Tel: 020 7607 1628; www.historicalpublications.co.uk)

ISBN 978-1-905286-33-1
British Library Cataloguing-in-Publication Data
A catalogue record for this book is available from the British Library

Typeset by Historical Publications Ltd
Reproduction by Tintern Graphics
Printed in Zaragoza, Spain by Edelvives

The Illustrations
The following have kindly given permission for reproduction of illustrations:

London Borough of Brent: *page 81*
London Borough of Camden:
*pages 10, 13, 14, 27 (left), 42, 45 (bottom), 46 (top), 48 (bottom), 54, 67, 75, 90, 95, 103, 107, 110
(bottom), 111 (both), 124, 129, 130, 137*
Marianne Colloms: *pages 50, 82*
The front cover is a watercolour by Mary Hill, c. 1930, of Perrin's Court.
The back cover is a 1936 oil painting by Charles Ginner, entitled Flask Walk Fifth November,
reproduced by kind permission of Richard Burrows and the photographer Janet Balmforth.
Other illustrations were supplied by Historical Publications Ltd

*It has not been possible to trace the next of kin/executors for Mary Hill. Any persons connected with her
and to whom any reproduction fees may be due should contact the publisher.*

Acknowledgements
The Author would like to thank the staff of Camden Local Studies and Archives for their help,
and also Christopher Wade for kindly looking over the manuscript and suggesting
some amendments.

The Hampstead Book

The A-Z of its history and people

Steven Denford

HISTORICAL PUBLICATIONS

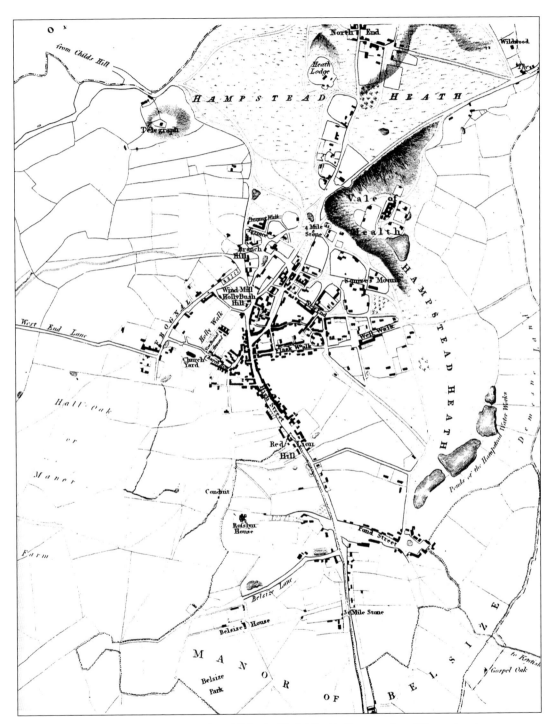

Map of Hampstead in 1814, published with J J Park's Topography of Hampstead.

Introduction

What is it about Hampstead? Words starting with H spring to mind – heath, hill and health. High on its hill, away above the dirt and smoke of the city, Hampstead has attracted visitors for centuries and many have chosen to stay. Initially praised for the quality of its air and the purity of its water – the Tudors sent their royal washing here – from the 18th century it became a centre of entertainment. First, it enjoyed two spells as a spa town, then in the 19th century came the Romantic artists and poets who extolled the virtues of its untamed Heath. The Heath, set about with fairground attractions on Bank Holidays, was later the big draw for poorer Londoners who came in droves once the railway had arrived and workers had the chance to enjoy some spare time. 'Appy 'Ampstead was born.

The popularity of the spa encouraged the extension of the village westwards on to Heath land – thus 'New' End came into being. The lower slopes of Hampstead, at South End and in Belsize, were later attractive to developers, when transport became easier. And once the Maryon Wilson family was free to exploit its lands the affluent area centred on Fitzjohn's Avenue was developed from the 1870s. It just needed the Underground stations at Hampstead and Belsize Park in 1907 to consolidate Hampstead's appeal.

Hampstead has a reputation for its artistic and intellectual residents. Not only was it the home of Keats and Constable, but the image was augmented from the 1930s by a more radical, avant-garde element, especially with the influx of refugees from Nazi oppression, men such as Gropius who influenced the design of the Isokon flats in Lawn Road, Sigmund Freud whose work was carried on by his daughter, and artists such as Mondrian who worked at the Mall Studios. During the 1930s Hampstead could be said to have been the centre of intellectual life in Britain.

Hampstead takes its name from an Anglo-Saxon word for a homestead or manor. The Anglo-Saxons were almost certainly the first people to live here permanently. In a charter, supposedly of 986AD and almost certain a forgery but probably based on an oral tradition, the land was given to the monks of Westminster.

Before Hampstead's absorption into the London Borough of Camden in 1965, its boundaries were virtually the same as they had been in Saxon times. The old Roman road that in our area is called Kilburn High Road and Shoot-up Hill is the western limit. To the north, east and south the bounds are less clear cut and are complicated to describe. Put briefly, old Hampstead stretches south to Boundary Road and to part of Primrose Hill, and on the east to Parliament Hill and the grounds of Kenwood. In the north Hampstead takes in part of Child's Hill and North End.

There have been many books on Hampstead, ranging from the young J J Park's volume of 1814, to Professor Thompson's thought-provoking book of 1974 on the physical development of the town. In between there was in 1912 the three volume, sumptuously illustrated, *Annals of Hampstead* by Thomas Barratt. In recent times there have been books by Christopher Wade, who with his wife Diana, founded the Hampstead Museum.

This present book in A-Z form deals with the history not just of the Hampstead of popular imagination, the left-leaning, affluent village on its hill, the spiritual home of the chattering classes. It encompasses too the outlying settlements such as Kilburn and West End, now unrecognisable as West Hampstead, and the other 'Ends' to the south and north. The format of the book enables the reader to look up a topic easily and the work is intended also as a companion for those walking and looking.

**Text in bold type
indicates a separate entry.**

Adelaide Road

Started by Eton College in 1830 as a turning westwards off **Haverstock Hill**, the road was named after William IV's newly crowned queen. The London & Birmingham Railway, first projected in 1831 and opened in 1837, discouraged development, which only began in 1839. The College demanded that the railway's Primrose Hill Tunnel *(see p. 99)* be so constructed that it could support houses on the top and it was driven through the London clay to a depth of 68 ft; the excavated material was used to raise the nearby Camden Goods Station. Well over a thousand feet long, it was London's first railway tunnel and crowds gathered along the empty Adelaide Road to watch its construction.

The road was built up with semi-detached houses; early plans for houses with mews were dropped and an omnibus service was opened along it in 1856, by when it had been driven through to Avenue and Finchley Roads.

A popular stop for omnibuses was the Adelaide Tavern, one of the first buildings in the street, at No.1. It burnt down in 1985. The road remained middle-class until after **World War One**, but its large houses were by then being converted to institutional use and from the 1930s demolished for flats. This process gathered pace after wartime bombing and the 1960s saw high rise development on the 33-acre **Chalcots** area of the Eton College Estate.

Famous people have lived in the road, albeit briefly. No.91

Adelaide Road, looking east towards Haverstock Hill c.1905.

was the home to the young William de Morgan (1839-1917) in 1855; No.43 to the painter Frank Topham (d. 1924) from 1882 to 1868, and the engraver William Holl (1808-71) was at No.174 in 1870-71. Similarly short stays were enjoyed by the painter Stanley Spencer and the writer Mary Webb.

Admiral's House

Since 1917 this intriguing house in Admiral's Walk has borne that name from a mistaken connection with Admiral Matthew Barton (1715-95), who actually lived at **Vane House**. The original house was built in 1700 by a vintner called Charles Keys, who called it Golden Spikes, probably after the symbol of the Masonic lodge that met there in the 1730s. It was known as The Grove when Fountain North, a naval captain first paid the rates in 1775. He lived here until he died in 1811 and it was he and not the Admiral who adapted the roof to look like a ship's deck; he even installed a couple of cannon up there, which he fired to celebrate naval victories or royal

The mistakenly-named Admiral's House in Admiral's Walk, 1796.

St Saviour's church in an astonishingly barren Eton Road, at the beginning of the 20th century. The architect was E M Barry. In the distance is Wellington House, designed by the sculptor Alfred Stevens (1817-75) for his own occupation but incomplete at his death. It is now replaced by flats. He lived from 1865 at the nearby No.9 Eton Villas.

birthdays. This practice inspired P L Travers to create Admiral Boom's house in *Mary Poppins*.

The architect Sir George Gilbert Scott (1811-78) rented the house from 1856 to 1864 when working on some of his best buildings, including the Albert Memorial; he also designed a gallery for the local **Christ Church**.

Adjoining Admiral's House at right angles is Grove Lodge, a building of about the same age and John Galsworthy's (1867-1933) last London home from 1918-33. During his stay here he completed *The Forsyte Saga* and won the Nobel Prize for literature.

Anglican Churches

The first Anglican place of worship outside **St John's parish church** was the **Well Walk** or Hampstead chapel, converted from the Great Room of the **Wells** in 1725. Although proprietary (i.e. privately owned) it was considered a chapel of ease and was hired by the parish when the church was being rebuilt or repaired. It was in continuous use until the congregation moved to its replacement, **Christ Church** in 1852; thereafter it was home to Presbyterians and then became the HQ of the **Hampstead Rifle Volunteers** before its demolition in 1882. Another proprietary chapel, and now the last of its kind in London, opened in 1823. St John's, **Downshire Hill** served a new area which had grown up south of Hampstead town.

Church building began in earnest in the 1850s as Hampstead spread. A respectable place of worship was very important in any new development. Hence churches such as St Peter's, Belsize Park, where the eccentric Dr Tremlett, a fanatical champion of the Confederates in the American Civil War, was vicar for over half a century, and St Saviour's, Eton Road, designed by E M Barry (1830-80), later architect of the Royal Opera House. Only Anglican places of worship were permitted on both the Belsize and Eton College estates.

In West Hampstead, with its smaller estates, the churches mainly began life as missions until support could be gathered for a permanent church. Holy Trinity on Finchley Road, however, had its origins in a temporary church put up in the fields at the foot of what became **Fitzjohn's Avenue**. That was replaced by a thatched-roofed iron church probably in 1859 (when it appears in the rate books). In the mid 1860s Rev. Henry Sharpe, fresh from the backwoods of Lake Ontario, undertook mission work from here among the navvies digging the Belsize railway tunnel, sometimes preaching sixty feet underground. He stayed on and was appointed the first minister of Holy Trinity when it opened in 1872.

Anglican ministries were particularly active in Hampstead in the Victorian period and, being less socially divided than elsewhere, were also more united in perceiving and facing their common threat, the desertion of the middle classes from organised Christianity. They were largely successful, for by 1903 over half of Hampstead's total church attendances were still Anglican, with Dissenters at just under 37 per cent.

'Appy 'Ampstead

'Appy 'Ampstead became a nationally known phrase in the 1890s, when celebrated in a song by Albert Chevalier and in the cartoons of Phil May. It refers to the Bank Holiday invasion of Hampstead by cockneys.

The opening of **Hampstead Heath station** in 1860 assured the Heath's future as a playground for East Enders. In 1863 Watkin Williams penned a music hall song, popularised by Miss Annie Adams, who sang "Hampstead is the place to ruralise, rit-rit-ruralise, extramuralise". The song was about a family excursion to the Heath, where they discover a toad in their teapot. Perhaps this was at the **Vale of Health**, where an informal fair had by then sprung up and a huge hotel had been built to profit from the crowds brought by the

railway. The trend was encouraged by the Lord of the Manor, Sir Thomas Maryon Wilson (1800-69), who, in his development battle with the local gentry, licensed an ice-cream vendor to build a wooden refreshment room at the foot of **Downshire Hill** in 1861 and assigned a large site for a fairground in 1865, renting out pitches.

Soon after the Heath became a public open space the Bank Holidays Act was passed, which created three holidays in months when it was possible to enjoy the Heath. Enormous crowds gathered, as on Whit Monday 1872, when the fair covered the whole of East Heath up to Spaniard's Road. The *Illustrated London News* described the fair as a "congregation of working class Londoners, everywhere swarming in multitudinous clusters …"

An organ grinder and his dancers on Hampstead Heath.

Damage, particularly fires among the furze, and rowdiness were often a problem in the 1870s, when there might be 30,000 visitors at the August holiday and 50,000 on a fine Whit Monday. Local residents were frequently harassed by holidaymakers demanding a drink of water and were relieved when Miss Crump erected a drinking fountain on **South End Green**.

Edward Walford (1823-97) writing at the time compared Hampstead to a seaside resort, with its donkeys, bath-chairs, fashionable esplanade, troops of visitors and houses and apartments to be let, and mentioned a comedy or farce called *Happy Hampstead* produced at the Royalty Theatre in 1877.

The opening of the tram along **Fleet Road** brought yet more working-class visitors. Every fine Sunday promenaders would throng Spaniards Road to enjoy the panoramic view over London. By 1910 there were fewer assaults and thefts but attendance on Easter Monday, always the Heath's busiest day, was estimated at 200,000. That year there appeared a music-hall song for Harry Champion (remembered for *I'm 'Enery the Eighth*, and *Boiled Beef and Carrots*):

On a holiday Monday to Hampstead you should go;
Everybody is up for fun, Fathers, mothers and everyone.
That's the place to see! The chaps and donahs dance;
You can have more fun on Hampstead Heath
Than you can in the South of France.

Hampstead Heath entered into Cockney rhyming slang as the word (i.e. 'Ampsteads) for

Annesley Lodge in Platts Lane, built 1895/6 by Charles Francis Annesley Voysey for his father.

teeth. The Bank Holiday fairs remained popular throughout the 20th century and into the new Millennium.

Architects and Builders

Hampstead has an extraordinary number of architect-designed houses, mainly in the districts that were developed from the 1870s on the Maryon Wilson land, around **Fitzjohn's Avenue** and later around Redington Road. Among architects who built in Hampstead, including several who built houses for themselves or their relatives, were Ewan Christian, Richard Norman Shaw, C F A Voysey, Erno Goldfinger, Reginald Blomfield, Banister Fletcher and Basil Champneys. In the 1930s Hampstead was a home of Modernism, with the construction of the **Isokon** flats, but architects of a different persuasion were residents of Hampstead at the time. Clough Williams-Ellis (1883-1978) lived at **Romney's House**, and built four houses in Ellerdale Close in 1934.

After the war examples of 'English Brutalism' appeared in **South Hill Park** by a number of architects designing for themselves, such as No.78 by Brian Housden in 1968. The modernist architect Sir Frederick Gibberd (1908-84) lived at No.49 Holford Road. The post-modernist Sir James Stirling (1924-92) lived at No.56 Belsize Avenue in the 1980s. At the same period Richard Rogers (b. 1933) lived at No.18 Belsize Grove and his rival Norman Foster (b. 1935) later lived at No.9 Hampstead Hill Gardens.

Most houses in Hampstead were created by builders, usually local men, working on a small scale from pattern books, but there were several working on a much larger scale. These included Batterbury & Huxley, William Willett, father and son, and the prolific Edward Jarvis Cave, whose red-brick shopping parades and blocks of mansion flats are everywhere to be seen. Although made bankrupt in 1900, he continued developments in the name of his wife Elizabeth.

Proposed Artists' Studios in Park(hill) Road c. 1880. The architect was T K Green.

Artists' Studios

John Constable and **Leigh Hunt** and his circle established Hampstead's reputation as an intellectual centre, and many artists were attracted to the wild beauty of the Heath and its light on the northern heights of London. There have been numerous studios, some purpose-built. **George Romney** had one of the very earliest. The studios built in about 1880 in Parkhill Road (then Park Road) have disappeared but many others have survived.

Thomas Batterbury (of Batterbury & Huxley) built several studios in the 1870s as well as several houses for artists in Steele's Road. Steele's Studios were to be home to C R W Nevinson (1889-1946), famous for his Vorticist paintings and Wychcombe Studios became the work-place

of the marine artist Norman Wilkinson. Batterbury's most famous studios were built in Tasker Road in 1872. At the Mall Studios, a stable-like terrace of cottages, an early occupant there was George Clausen (1852-1944) and in the early 1900s Arthur Rackham (1867-1939) and Walter Sickert (1860-1942) were here, but its most significant period was in the 1930s. Hampstead was then at the forefront of the arts and the Mall Studios housed an internationally-known group of artists. This included Barbara Hepworth (1903-75) and her second husband Ben Nicholson (1898-1986), and later Henry Moore (1894-1982). Moholy-Nagy and Naum Gabo, both residents of the **Isokon** flats, were frequent visitors as was Piet Mondrian (1872-1944) who lived at No.60

Parkhill Road. In 1938 Alexander Calder (1898-1976), most famous for mobiles, gave a performance of *Circus* in Cecil Stephenson's studio.

No.14A **Downshire Hill** was used as studios by the Carline family during the First World War and Nevinson and Mark Gertler (1891-1939), who also worked at the Penn Studio off Rudall Crescent, came there. Richard Carline (1896-1980) was co-founder of the Hampstead Artists' Council in 1944. The house later became the headquarters of the Artists' Refugee Committee. Sir Roland Penrose, the art expert, who lived in Downshire Hill, was also responsible for bringing refugees to Hampstead, including many expelled after the closure of the Bauhaus in 1933.

The **West Hampstead**

Studios in Sherriff Road were built from 1885 by Thomas Aitchison, a local builder. The twin brothers Maurice and Edward Detmold, animal and bird painters who illustrated *The Jungle Book,* worked here in the early 1900s when their work was in great demand. Both were to commit suicide, although some fifty years apart. West Hampstead Studios was also the name of nearby No.165 Broadhurst Gardens, now used by English National Opera, but formerly the Decca recording studios. Here the Beatles had their failed audition for Decca Records on 1 January 1962. Dick Rowe became the laughing stock of the industry as "the man who turned down the Beatles", although George Harrison subsequently recommended he sign the Rolling Stones, which helped restore his reputation.

Assembly Rooms

The 19th-century Hampstead Assembly Rooms, near the top of **Holly Bush Hill**, consisted of the house built by George **Romney** and adjacent properties. It was conveyed to trustees in 1806, the money coming from a tontine lottery. The following year they leased a cottage and Romney's old stables for 21 years to Thomas Lovelock. He put up a new building, thereby creating the Holly Bush tavern, which for a time served as the Assembly Rooms' catering wing.

The Assembly Rooms became a cultural centre for Hampstead. Monthly meetings were held at which resident artistic and literary celebrities used to lend works of art. In 1829 the first Heath Protection meeting, chaired by James Fenton of nearby **Fenton**

George Romney's old house and adjacent buildings, converted into Assembly Rooms. In this drawing by A R Quinton in 1910, they are occupied by the Hampstead Constitutional Club.

House, took place here. In the early Victorian period the Hampstead Conversazione Society met at the Assembly Rooms, which remained in use, latterly more as a public hall than as an elegant social centre, until the opening in 1878 of the new Vestry hall in Haverstock Hill.

Avenue Road

This road was not developed until after the **Finchley Road** Act of 1826. Colonel Eyre was then able to open up his **St John's Wood** estate and link it to Regent's Park with a grand avenue. The boundary between the old parishes of Hampstead and St Marylebone is marked by two stones in Radlett Place. Most of the road's original buildings have gone. William Collins (1788-1847), the landscape painter, lived at No.20 **Avenue Road** from 1839-40. William's son Wilkie set one of the scenes of his novel *The Woman in White*, published in 1862 but based on childhood recollections, at the turnpike at Swiss Cottage. Sir Alexander

Korda (1893-1956), the film producer, lived at No.81 in the 1930s and other 20th-century residents of this area have included actors Matheson Lang and Sir Cedric Hardwicke. North of Adelaide Road, in what was originally called Upper Avenue Road, is the **Swiss Cottage Centre**. At the corner with College Crescent stood from the 1860s until World War Two the ornate school of the London Society for Teaching and Training the Blind.

Thomas Barratt

The most celebrated archivist of Hampstead, Thomas James Barratt (1841–1914), was notorious in his day as the instigator of modern advertising methods. Born at No.25 Tottenham Place, St Pancras, the son of a piano maker, he joined the soap-making business of A and F Pears in 1864, soon becoming a partner after marrying the boss's daughter. Thereafter, his life work was to expand the firm through increased

The dining room in Arts and Crafts style at a house called The Poplars, in Avenue Road. It was designed by J M Brydon (1840-1901), who lived in Steele's Road.

advertising, making Pears a household name throughout the English-speaking world. He boosted its image by publishing *Pears Cyclopaedia* and creating the Pears' Pictures for People, which offered high-quality reproductions of art works at a nominal price. The most famous of these was the portrait of a child by Sir John Everett Millais, distributed by Barratt under the title *Bubbles*.

Barratt was just as energetic in his other pursuits. He started a programme to buy open lands for preservation against development, a scheme which he urged others to emulate. He was passionately interested in microscopy, becoming a fellow of the Royal Microscopical Society.

But his local fame is as a historian. He made a lifelong collection of Hampsteadiana which he bequeathed to the municipality, and compiled the monumental, three-volume *Annals of Hampstead*, now a collector's item.

In 1880 Barratt combined four of the houses opposite **Whitestone Pond** into one house, which he called Bellmoor after one of them. Here he lived in grand style surrounded by his substantial collection of British art. The house contained a stunning, tiled Moorish room. A Tudor-style block of flats replaced his home in 1929.

Baths

The **Wells and Campden Trust** opened baths and washhouses at two sites in Hampstead during the 1880s. Both were designed by the Trust's

The main Hampstead baths and washhouses in Finchley Road before the Swiss Cottage baths were erected. The site was later occupied by Sainsbury's.

A magnificent photograph of Thomas Barratt, businessman, publicist, philanthropist and collector of Hampstead material.

Belsize

Belsize means 'beautifully situated', from the French *Bel Assis*. The name appears in a variety of forms until the early 18th century when the current spelling began to find favour. An estate within the manor of Hampstead, Belsize's existence was not recorded until 1317, when Sir Roger le Brabazon left a "messuage and fifty-seven acres of land in Hampstede" to Westminster Abbey. Sir Roger was Lord Chief Justice to Edward II, and the first of Belsize's absentee landlords. He left all this land to the monks of Westminster in return for masses to be said for his soul. In 1360, when it was owned by the prior Nicholas of Litlington, Belsize was discharged from all rents and services that were due to Hampstead manor in recognition of his benefactions to the abbey.

Belsize was surrendered to the king in 1540 and in 1542 was among the endowments of the newly constituted dean and chapter of Westminster, confirmed by Elizabeth I in 1560. Except during the Civil War period it remained with the dean and chapter until 1887, when the Church Commissioners took over. The freehold was sold off mostly to the sitting tenants of individual houses, mainly in the 1950s.

The estate was leased by the dean and chapter. The first lessee was Armigell Waad, Clerk of the Council to Henry VIII and Edward VI. He had been among the first of his countrymen to discover America, part of the 1536 expedition to Newfoundland, when famine, according to Hakluyt, led to cannibalism. He retired to **Belsize House**,

architect, Henry Legg. The first, in the west, was opened in Palmerston Road in June 1886 and the second on **Flask Walk** in September 1888. Cold baths cost one penny, warm baths twopence, the same price as use of a laundry tub and drying facilities. Indoor plumbing was a rarity at that time. They were both run at a loss and the Trust was able to persuade the Council to take them on in 1908. The Palmerston Road baths were shut in 1976 after a large explosion in the building. The Flask Walk Baths closed two years later and were converted into flats.

The local authority had built its own baths at around the same time. In 1887 the Swiss Cottage Skating Rink at No.177 Finchley Road gave way to Hampstead's first Public Baths and Gymnasium. These closed in 1964 when the swimming baths transferred to the new **Swiss Cottage Centre**. Sainsbury's was built on the site in 1973.

where he died in 1567. From 1683 for over a century the lease was held by the Earls of Chesterfield before they sold their interest to a syndicate of four local men, and the estate was then divided up into a number of separate leases. Modern-day **Belsize Park** was developed on the land from the 1850s.

Belsize Boxing Club

Belsize boxing club was formed in 1880, "to help protect local ladies", and trained for nearly 50 years across the Marylebone boundary at the Eyre Arms. Possibly the oldest amateur boxing club in the country, it was revived in 1965 and was allowed to use the British Boxing Board of Control's new gymnasium behind the **Load of Hay** on **Haverstock Hill**, which was for a few years renamed the Noble Art. In 1966 Muhammad Ali trained here in the run-up to the second of his two fights against British boxing legend Henry Cooper.

Belsize Court

In 1811 George Todd, a Baltic merchant, replaced an earlier mansion known in 1714 as the White House with an equally large house near today's Wedderburn Road. This enjoyed various names until it finally became Belsize Court. Its most notable occupant, from 1833 to 1869, was the self-made entrepreneur Matthew Forster, city merchant and MP for Berwick-on-Tweed until he was unseated by a bribery scandal. At the turn of the 20th century Arthur Rubinstein (1887-1982) often played at musical parties given by the oil magnate John Bergheim. The property was sold by the Church Commissioners in 1937 and

An 18th-century view of Belsize House, at the junction of today's Belsize Avenue, Belsize Park and Belsize Park Gardens.

replaced by five low-rise blocks of flats, also named Belsize Court.

Belsize House

There was a house on Belsize 'manor' from the early 14th century, probably rebuilt in brick on a much larger scale in 1496, when the Abbey muniments reveal production of 400,000 bricks at **Belsize**. It was the only aristocratic house of any size in Hampstead before the 16th century. It was rebuilt in 1663 by Colonel Daniel O'Neill, Gentleman of the Bedchamber to Charles II, at vast expense a year before he died of "an ulcer in the guts". His stepson, Lord Wotton, inherited and further improved the property, probably using the younger of the Tradescant family to develop the gardens. In August 1668 Samuel Pepys recorded in his diary that the gardens were "too good for the house...the most noble that ever I saw". The house was assessed in 1670s at 36 hearths, the largest in Hampstead by far. The house and grounds feature in a 1696 painting by Jan Siberecht at Tate Britain.

After Lord Wotton's death in 1683, Belsize passed to his half-brother Philip, second Earl of Chesterfield, but he never lived there and from about 1704 sub-let the property on a series of life-leases. The first lessee was the notorious Charles Povey, a belligerent coal merchant, who was accused of selling off its fitments and bricks from the surrounding walls and despoiling the grounds. He published pamphlets against all who offended him, and threatened Chesterfield with a pamphlet if he insisted on taking him to law.

Povey opened Belsize House and gardens to the public, with five-shilling weddings available at a private chapel provided the feast took place in the grounds. In 1720 he further sub-let Belsize to the wily James Howell, self-styled 'His Excellency the Welsh Ambassador'. At a time when the first Hampstead spa was losing favour, Belsize rose to the height of its fame as pleasure gardens, without even a hint of medicinal waters. Open from 6am to 8pm, it offered music, dancing, gambling, and various novelties:

footmen races, evening duck hunts and twice-weekly deer hunts with venison 'ordinaries' or feasts. There were plenty of secluded arbours for other more flirtatious pleasures. The management also provided guests with a sturdy patrol back to London. In 1721, the future George II and his wife dined at the house and the following year there was an attendance of between 300 and 400 carriages. But, as Barratt wrote, Belsize became "over-boisterous and lost its manners, polite society declined to be drawn by its coarse attractions". As early as 1722 Belsize was satirised as a venue that had "publicly become a rendezvous, of strumpets, common as in common Stews…". Howell was accused of profiting from a "scandalous lewd house", and unlawful gaming was suppressed. Although the fashionable patrons deserted it, entertainments, including music and athletics, continued at Belsize into the 1740s.

The dean and chapter of Westminster permitted Chesterfield to pull down and replace the ruinous manor house; a new lessee did so. The unfortunate future prime minister Spencer Perceval rented this new Belsize House and its the park from 1797 to 1808. He considered it "a miserable hole". It was rebuilt in about 1812 and by 1841 was described as an elegant mansion that included a Gothic conservatory, vineries, aviaries, and a Grecian temple.

After the break-up of the Belsize estate in 1808 the house and its pentagon-shaped grounds, stretching from **Haverstock Hill** to **College Crescent**, were occupied by tenants. The final tenant was the retired wine merchant Sebastian Gonzalez Martinez. Demolition followed in the autumn of 1853. The site of the house is at the junction of Belsize Avenue, Belsize Park, and Belsize Park Gardens. The last was built over the carriage drive and the mulberry tree by No.1 is a survivor from the garden.

Belsize Park

The name of a street begun in the 1850s but it is also applied to the surrounding area. Now regarded as a smart London suburb, not so long ago Belsize Park was an area of multiple occupation in bedsits in large houses. A strong Area Conservation Committee and an equally thriving Belsize Residents' Association have helped its transformation into an affluent district, as it was when first developed.

The Earl of Chesterfield had sold off the 234 acres of the **Belsize** land in 1808 to clear his debts. It was split up into a number of smaller estates centred on new or existing large houses. This dictated the street layout when building began, on no overall plan, in the 1850s.

The **Belsize House** estate was sold in 1852 to Charles James Palmer, who got into financial difficulties and the dean and chapter converted the lease into separate 99-year leases for individual dwellings as each was completed, to

Some development on the Belsize estate is shown on this map of the early 1860s. Adelaide Road and the railway are at the bottom.

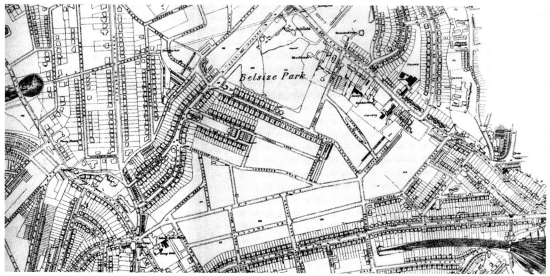

Palmer's nominee, usually the builder Daniel Tidey. **Belsize Village** was created on this estate. East of Haverstock Hill, **St John's Park** was developed mainly in the 1860s on the grounds of Haverstock Lodge. Fringing the west side of Haverstock Hill were two large 19th-century houses called Hillfield and Woodlands, both estates owned by the Woodd family, known locally for their benevolent and public-spirited attitude. This was the last part of Belsize Park to be developed, in the Edwardian period.

To the north lay the estate of **Rosslyn House**, which Henry Davidson retained as his home while planning a good-class extension to Hampstead town from 1853. Development of Rosslyn Park, as it became known, was slow perhaps because builders were wary of the Midland railway tunnel built beneath it in 1868.

Most of the main thoroughfares of Belsize Park were built up by 1866, and the professional middle-class populated the new district. By 1900, Belsize Park was much as it appears today. There are few survivals from its more rural past but one, on ancient Belsize Lane, is the charming castellated cottage orné, Hunters Lodge, built in 1811.

Belsize Park Station

The Underground station was opened in 1907 as part of the **Hampstead Tube** and retains its original appearance. It became a popular air raid shelter in the last war, and its sleeping shelterers were the inspiration for a famous series of sketches by Henry Moore, who wrote that "I had never seen so many reclining figures, and even the train tunnels

Belsize Park Underground station soon after it opened in 1907. To the left of the picture is a signboard indicating the premises of the Russell nursery grounds.

seemed to be like the holes in my sculptures".

By 1942 a Deep Shelter was constructed beneath the Tube platforms, whose massive access shafts remain clearly visible above ground; it still has its 9,000 steel bunk beds in place, many now used for archives storage. When open, compressed air was used to lift waste (human and otherwise) up to the level of the main sewer system. The Belsize Park Deep Shelter and others beneath several other underground stations in London were planned to be linked up after the war to form express lines, but funds were not forthcoming.

Belsize Village

The name is an invention of mid-Victorian developers. It is centred on the junction of Belsize Lane with the pedestrianised Belsize Terrace, built over the farm of **Belsize House**. The farmhouse stood half-way down Belsize Lane and the farmer charged a toll of one penny to passing traffic. A much repeated story tells that when Queen Victoria drove

down Belsize Lane one day, the farmer's daughter, left in charge, demanded the toll. On this occasion, the queen was amused and paid up.

In November 1856 the builder Daniel Tidey started a short terrace comprising Belsize tavern and three shops, but then went bankrupt; when he was discharged two years later he extended it. The developer William Willett senior (1837-1913) gave up land to open up the triangular Belsize 'village green', which later evolved into a service zone for the grander homes in neighbouring streets, with a set of mews for servants and horses. Today, this is a charming spot, much loved by local residents. It has enough small shops to give a village feel and is now smartly paved.

Leading north is Belsize Crescent, which contains at No.6 Willett senior's first house in Hampstead; he was to build many, many more. Lesley Hornby, alias Twiggy, lived at No.20 before she became a top model. To the south-west, No.41 Belsize Park was Jerome K Jerome's (1859-1927) last home, to which he moved in

Belsize Village in 2009.

Branch Hill

An old branch route to **Child's Hill**. Its pond dried up before World War One but featured in many of **Constable's** paintings. Opposite the pond site, The Chestnuts, was for most of the 1930s the family home of the famous American bass Paul Robeson (1898-1976).

The original Branch Hill Lodge was known in the early 18th century as Bleak Hall as well as Judges' Bench House. It has had many associations with lawyers, notably Alexander Wedderburn (1733-1805), here until 1794. Wedderburn, then called Lord Loughborough, was known as 'the second Judge Jeffreys' for his treatment of the 1780 Gordon Rioters, who were condemned to be hanged by the score, regardless of age.

In the early 19th century a wealthy merchant Thomas Neave, enlarged the house,

1924. To the south-east, in Belsize Park Gardens, Lytton Strachey (1880-1932) reluctantly stayed at two different houses, including No.6 where he wrote much of his *Eminent Victorians*. The marine artist Clarkson Stanfield (1793-1867) had died at the house in 1867. No.44 has a blue plaque to the composer Frederick Delius (1862-1934), who lived here in 1918-19 at the height of his career. In the 1930s, No.37 was the home of Jack Pritchard (1899-1992), art-loving industrialist, who founded the **Isokon** furniture firm.

Branch Hill, from the drawing by W Westall, published in 1829.

Branch Hill Lodge; lithograph by Thomas Way.

Ford Madox Brown's painting 'Work' depicting sewer works at The Mount on the west of Heath Street, a canvas not finished until 1868.

which he filled with stained glass from convents plundered during the French Revolution, in addition to the commemorative window taken from the **Chicken House**. Lady Byron rented the house shortly after her separation from the poet. The present house dates from 1868, but was rebuilt in 1901 and turned into an old people's home in the mid 1960s, when the estate was purchased by Camden. The old kitchen garden (below the neo-Gothic gatehouse) has been preserved for the public as allotments, but the rest of the sloping grounds were developed in 1978 with 42 paired houses. At the time they were said to be the most expensive Council houses ever built, costing on average £70,000. The development was called Spedan Close, after the neighbouring Spedan Tower, a stately home built in 1889 by the store-owner John (Spedan) Lewis who died there aged 93 in 1928. His mansion was demolished to build the grandiose Firecrest development in the 1980s.

Ford Madox Brown

The painter Ford Madox Brown (1821-93) eloped in 1848 with a fifteen-year-old country girl and installed her in a small house in Hampstead. He kept her a secret from his friends in the Pre-Raphaelite Brotherhood for some years while he educated her to the required standard, carrying out a sort of correspondence course with her in Hampstead, including advice about handling the local tradesmen. In 1852, he came to live briefly in the town, probably at No.33 **High Street**, on the later site of the Blue Star Garage. He started his famous painting *Work*, inspired by the sight of navvies at work on Hampstead's sewers in The Mount, **Heath Street**.

Madox Brown valued the dignity of labour. He felt that "the British excavator... was at least as worthy of the powers of an English painter as the fisherman of the Adriatic, the peasant of the Campagna or the Neapolitan lazzarone". The picture depicts an allegory of different types of worker and non-worker, the idle rich on horseback and the idle poor, out-of-work haymakers lying beyond the railings. On the right are two brainworkers, portraits of F D Maurice (hatless) and Thomas Carlyle. The larger version of the picture, not finally completed until 1868, is now in the Manchester Art Gallery and was reproduced in **Barratt**'s *Annals of Hampstead*. Madox Brown spent many weeks sitting in Heath Street, drawing and painting the background to the astonishment of passers-by. The details of Heath Street seem to be topographically accurate; most of the houses shown in The Mount and Mount Square have changed little since Madox Brown recorded them.

The painter's final visit to Hampstead appears to have been in 1883, when he stayed in Holly Cottage, now No.12, The Mount (in the background of *Work*).

Burgh House during its period of occupation by the Royal East Middlesex Militia, 1858-c.1881.

Burgh House

Grade I Listed Burgh House in New End Square was built in 1703 as Brook House by Henry and Hannah Sewell, wealthy Quakers, and greatly extended after 1720 by Dr William Gibbons, physician to Hampstead **Wells**, who died here in 1728. He probably erected its handsome wrought-iron gates which bear his initials. He praised Hampstead's water (somewhat equivocally) and was possibly responsible for making mahogany furniture fashionable in Britain.

From 1822 until his death in 1856 the owner was Rev. Allatson Burgh, vicar of St Lawrence Jewry in the City. Burgh neglected his flock and the house, despite giving it its present name. From 1858 to about 1881, Burgh House was the Officers' Mess of the Royal East Middlesex Militia, with additional barracks built either side of the parade ground created in the front garden.

Later residents included the stained glass painter Thomas Grylls, whose firm designed the rose window above Poets' Corner at Westminster Abbey and Dr George Williamson, who commissioned Gertrude Jekyll to design the garden. From 1925 to 1934 the owner was Captain Constantine Benson who added the impressive music room, with panelling from the Long Room of the Wells. The last private owners of the house were Captain George Bambridge and his wife Elsie, daughter of the writer Rudyard Kipling, who visited them here. Upon Kipling's death in 1937, the couple used their inheritance to purchase Wimpole Hall in Cambridgeshire, now owned by the National Trust.

Empty during **World War Two**, Burgh House was acquired in 1946 by Hampstead Borough Council, who turned it into a community centre. It was closed in 1977 for conversion into offices, but saved for community use after a strong local campaign, led by among others the barrister, David Sullivan. It was leased in 1979 to the Burgh House Trust, which runs it as a community and arts centre; it includes a café, an art gallery and the **Hampstead Museum** of local history.

Camden Arts Centre

At the foot of the Arkwright Road, Camden Arts Centre was built in 1897 as Hampstead's first Central Public Library. The building, designed in domestic Tudor style by Arnold Tayler, was twice bombed in **World War Two** *(see pp 83 & 137)*. The library transferred to **Swiss Cottage** in 1964 and the council converted the building into an exhibition and teaching centre with floor space of 5,000 square feet. At first, the Centre was co-operatively run by the Hampstead Artists Council and borough council staff, notching up many notable exhibitions.

However, the building had structural disadvantages and following a refurbishment by Tony Fretton Architects, Camden Arts Centre re-opened to the public in 2004, combining the original features with a contemporary design to enhance space and light. A broad range of work is displayed including installation, film and video, light sensitive drawings and sculpture.

Camden History Society

The Camden History Society was founded in 1970 and since 1973 has published the annual *Camden History Review*. It promotes interest in the history of all parts of the borough of Camden. It has a programme of lectures, and a bi-monthly newsletter. Over the years it has undertaken much detailed research into the history of Hampstead, and produced numerous publications, including three surveys covering each street within the area of this book.

Cannon Hall, home of the du Mauriers. Drawing by A R Quinton, 1911.

Cannon Hall

Stately Cannon Hall (No.14 Cannon Place) dates from about 1720. It was originally called Rous's Buildings, probably after Joseph Rous, who succeeded John Duffield as lessee of the Wells estate. In mid century Cannon Hall was occupied by Sarah **Holford** of the prominent Hampstead family. The cannon (objects and name) were contributed by Sir James Cosmo Melville, Secretary to the East India Company, who lived at the Hall from 1838. It was the home from 1916-34 of Daphne **du Maurier**'s actor-manager father, Sir Gerald. In the garden wall of Cannon Hall, on Cannon Lane, is the ancient lock-up, in use from about 1730 for a century. Here suspected criminals were kept in much discomfort before being charged.

Capo di Monte

This delightful two-storey cottage orné at the top of Windmill Hill overlooks the West Heath and comprises two or three cottages knocked into one. Sarah Siddons (1755-1831), leading actress of her day, stayed here in 1804-05 for her health. In the 1940s architectural and art historian Sir Kenneth Clark (1903-83) lived here briefly but found it too small and in 1943 moved across the lane to Upper Terrace House in Upper Terrace. From 1949, Capo di Monte was the home of the novelist, critic and broadcaster Marghanita Laski (1915-88).

Central School of Speech and Drama

The school was founded in 1906 by Elsie Fogerty, a specialist in speech training,

The actress, Sarah Siddons, resident of Capo di Monte.

The Hampstead Conservatoire in Eton Avenue, c. 1905, now the home of the Central School of Speech and Drama.

and fifty years later moved from its home in the Royal Albert Hall to its present site in Eton Avenue.

The original building, much of which survives, was built in 1888 as the Hampstead Conservatoire of Music and School of Art. The Conservatoire prospered under the direction of the folk music enthusiast Cecil Sharp from 1896 to 1905. It was used for lectures and concerts, and possessed a Willis organ that was moved in 1910 to Brighton parish church. By 1906 the Conservatoire had been amalgamated with the London Academy of Music, but closed in the 1920s.

In 1929 the Embassy Theatre opened in its adapted building, with the Embassy School of Acting formed in 1933. Damaged in the war the building was restored and reopened in 1945 but the location of the theatre did not encourage large audiences and it closed in 1955.

The Central School moved in and flourished on its new site. In 1989 it was incorporated as a higher education college in its own right and funded directly by government. During the 1990s extensive building took place, with a modernist extension (1997) by Cullum & Nightingale, and in 2002 a refurbished Embassy Theatre was opened as part of the School. From September 2005 the Central became a College of the University of London, finally realising the ambitions of its founder.

Chalcots

First named in 1253, the Chalcots estate originated in a grant of one hide of land (possibly 120 acres) in Hampstead to the leper hospital of St James, Westminster (on the site of today's St James's Palace). Its property was given by Henry VI to his new Eton College in 1449. When Henry VIII exchanged property with Eton in 1531, Chalcots was expressly reserved to the college. The name means a shelter for travellers from cold weather and became corrupted to Chalk Farm. This was the name of an old tavern, previously Lower Chalcots Farm, at the south of the estate, which stretched from Belsize almost to the present Regent's Park Road (across the boundary with St Pancras).

Chalcots or Chalk Farm was treated by the College like its other estates. Statutes forbad land to be let for longer than 21 years, and in practice a lessee was expected to renew before expiry and pay a substantial fine. Fines were simply divided between Fellows and never shown in College accounts, so Fellows felt no great incentive to develop the land. Nevertheless development began in the 1830s, described under the **Eton College Estate**.

In 1842 the College acquired 32 acres of Crown land in Eton in exchange for 53 acres of the southern portion of Chalcots, which became **Primrose Hill** public open space. The rest of Chalcots was covered in housing in the course of the 19th century. In 1995 the College decided to pull out of the Chalcots estate and sold over 1,000 of its residential properties for little more than £4 million. The new landlords of the 1300 flats and 140 houses, a consortium of Compco and Southend Property Holdings, became the biggest freeholders in Hampstead.

Chicken House

Nos.54-66 Rosslyn Hill stand on the site of this oddly-named house. Chicken House was a Jacobean building, reputedly once a hunting lodge. This contained a remarkable stained-glass window (removed to **Branch Hill** Lodge) showing portraits of James I (r. 1603-23) and his favourite, the Duke of Buckingham (1592-1628), with a French inscription stating that they stayed the night here on 25 August 1619. It became a

Portraits of James I and his favourite the Duke of Buckingham, in a window at the Chicken House, Rosslyn Hill. Drawing by W P Sherlock.

tavern and in the later 18th century a lodging-house much patron-ised by lawyers, among whom was William Murray, the future Lord Mansfield. In 1815 it was in a state of dilapidation, the front disfigured by tenements, and by the time it was demolished in 1880 it was locally described as a den of thieves.

Child's Hill

A district on both sides of the Finchley Road and the Hendon-Hampstead border, Child's Hill took its name from Richard le Child, who in 1312 had a house and 30 acres probably on the Hendon side. In 1784 there was a freehold estate of 57 acres called Hogman's farm, which was divided up at the end of the 18th century. The house and surrounding six acres were held after 1810 by the Platt family, including Thomas Pell Platt (d.1852), an oriental scholar who translated the Bible into Ethiopian. He gave his name to the nearby lane from West End and Fortune Green to the Heath. At the north end of Platt's Lane lies Telegraph Hill, named after the signalling station that was based here during the Napoleonic wars.

The area's isolation was lessened in 1830 by the formation of **Finchley Road**. West of the road a house called Temple Park was built by Henry Weech Burgess, a prosperous Lancastrian, and to the east **Kidderpore Hall** was built in 1843. Building on the estate owned by Burgess commenced in 1878 and around Kidderpore Hall in the years after 1890. Childs Hill House and its estate was sold for building in 1896, and Rosecroft Avenue laid across the land.

The development of Child's Hill was complete by 1913. A significant building is No.8 Platt's Lane *(see illustration on page 9)*, designed in 1896 by the architect C F A Voysey (1857-1941) for his father Rev. Charles Voysey, who had been expelled from his living in Yorkshire for heresy having denied the existence of Hell and questioned the divinity of Christ. An L-shaped, roughcast house with sloping buttresses, Pevsner called it "astonishingly ahead of its date". It was originally known as Annesley Lodge (from one of Voysey's Christian names); it is now divided up. Nearby at No.21 is a private plaque to Thomas Masaryk (1850-1937), who lived here in exile during World War One, and was to become the first president of the newly independent Czechoslovakia.

Child's Hill village, c.1906.

Christ Church

Its spire a landmark for miles around, Christ Church was built to replace the crowded chapel in **Well Walk**. The patron of the parish church, Sir Thomas Maryon Wilson, was vigorously opposed, since half of the potential congregation, many of the wealthiest in Hampstead, were to be included in the new district, hence a substantial reduction in income for the incumbent of the parish church. Maryon Wilson was also deeply suspicious of the **Hoare** family and their friends who were sponsoring the new church, while preventing him from developing his Hampstead estate.

Nevertheless, the church opened on freehold land, part of the former workhouse garden, in 1852. Most of the nearly £10,000 costs were met by the Hoares and the congregation was mainly rich.

The original architect was

Christ Church in Hampstead Square, by A R Quinton 1910.

Samuel Dawkes, but the west gallery, now removed, was designed in 1860 by George Gilbert Scott, who worshipped here.

Church Row

The handsomest street in Hampstead. In Georgian times it was the most famous promenade north of the Thames and its elegance is almost completely preserved today. Nearly all the houses are of early-18th-century origin, with flush-framed windows, and are Listed II*. Their overall lack of uniformity in width, height and design adds to the street's charm.

Eight houses on the south side were built in 1713 by Richard Hughes of Holborn as a speculation stimulated by the success of the **Wells**. In the survey of 1762 the north side of Church Row had ten houses of various dates from the early 18th century. The two sides of the row are not quite parallel and the road has long been divided by trees.

New trees were presented to Church Row in 1876 by three architects living at Nos.20, 24 and 26 respectively: Thomas Garner, G F Bodley and George Gilbert Scott Jr. Another architect in Scott's office, Temple Moore, helped to plant

Church Row by A R Quinton in 1910. Looking west to the parish church of St John, a view hardly changed today, except for cars parked on either side. The trees in the centre are presumably those presented to the street in 1876 by three architects who lived there, Thomas Garner, G F Bodley and George Gilbert Scott jnr.

them, but all have now gone. In 1998 a new tree was added to the central reservation to celebrate the centenary of the **Heath and Hampstead Society** the previous year.

There have been many eminent residents in Church Row. On the north side, No.8 was the home of two once famous writers: Anna Barbauld (1743-1825), whose husband was a minister at Rosslyn Hill Chapel, and her niece, Lucy Aikin (1781-1864).

On the south side, at No.17 the historian Edward Walford (1823-97), who completed *Old and New London*, lived from 1860 to 1886; H G Wells (1866-1946) from 1909 to 1912; and the comedian Peter Cook (1937-1995) around 1970. No.18 has a plaque to John James Park,

who wrote the first history of Hampstead in 1814, and to his father, who must have advised him, as J J was only nineteen at the time. The artist, Margaret Gillies (1803-87), lived at No.25 for many years, following the death of her partner Dr Southwood Smith.

George Gilbert Scott Jr's son, Giles (1880-1960), the future architect of Liverpool Anglican Cathedral, was born at No.26. Later celebrities here included 'Bosie', Lord Alfred Douglas (1870-1945), who moved here in 1907, after winning a libel suit against the *Daily News* which had run an obituary calling him a degenerate only to find him still alive. In the 1950s Ludovic Kennedy and his wife ballerina Moira Shearer (1926-2006) lived at the

house. No.27 was the home of George du Maurier (1834-96), whose son, (Sir) Gerald, was born here in 1873, and during World War One of the folk song and dance expert, Cecil Sharp (1859-1924). The novelist Compton Mackenzie (1883-1972) lived at No.28 in 1910. It had previously been the office of the Women's Co-operative Guild, visited by Virginia Woolf, who described the "immaculate and moral heights of Hampstead".

The Hampstead Reformatory School for Girls, founded in 1857, occupied the large No.9 until 1876 when it moved to **East Heath Road**. Their former home was then occupied by girls from the Field Lane Refuge.

Oriel House on the north side of Church Row, early 20th century. Watercolour by Frederick Adcock.

The former Grange cinema in Kilburn High Road, 1999.

Cinemas

The first moving pictures shown in Hampstead were probably at Fred Gray's fairground in the **Vale of Health** using a hand-held projector, although a moving picture show was recalled as having been held in about 1901 at the YMCA's premises in Willoughby Road. The first true cinema opened in 1910 at No.64 Heath Street, which had been converted for the New Eldorado Company. Variously known as the Eldorado and the Hampstead Picture Palace, it became tea rooms in 1916.

Two other cinemas opened in 1910 in **Kilburn**, both with a similarly short life but the Kilburn Grange cinema, seating 1,300 at the corner of Messina Avenue, which opened in 1914 lasted until 1977, when it became a nightclub. Another early cinema in this area was the Maida Vale Palace, just inside the borough boundary, which in 1927 was fitted with a Grand Wurlitzer so powerful that neighbours tried to block the cinema's licence. It seated 1,500 and had palatial fittings. In 1961 it became the first commercial bingo hall in the country, and is now an Islamic centre. The **Kilburn Empire** was a full-time cinema from 1928 and after several changes of name eventually closed in 1981.

Hampstead Picture Playhouse, a 'luxurious hall' in **Pond Street** close to the tram terminus and railway, was opened in August 1913 and drew large audiences. The original owners were concerned to stress that "no questionable films will be shown on the premises". It was refurbished as a three-screen cinema in 1986 but closed in November 2000, when it was the longest surviving cinema in Camden. Its site is now taken by a Marks & Spencer store.

Oscar Deutsch opened two outlets in Hampstead during the 1930s. The Odeon in **Swiss Cottage** was then his grandest venture; it was converted into a three-screen cinema in 1973 but is still going strong. The

Odeon on **Haverstock Hill** was in operation until 1972. Five years after it closed the smaller Screen on the Hill was opened next door. It is now a small branch of Hampstead's most famous cinema, the **Everyman**.

In the last few years an eight-screen multiplex cinema has opened in the O_2 centre on Finchley Road.

College Crescent

This College refers not to Eton but to a theological training establishment for Non-conformists. This was the imposing, turreted New College that was built together with much of the Crescent in 1851. It was the first place of worship for Congregationalists in the parish, and was affiliated to the University of London's school of divinity from 1900. Dissenting divinity students were enabled to enjoy an Oxbridge-style education. It was united in 1924 with the Hackney Theological College at No.527 **Finchley Road** and ten years later the students moved there and the College and much of College Crescent were demolished and replaced by Northways, two concrete blocks of flats and shops.

The imposing No.40, built in 1881, was, at the turn of the 20th century, Northcourt, the home of Samuel Palmer, of Huntley & Palmer's biscuits. His family presented the elaborate drinking fountain at the corner with Fitzjohn's Avenue in his memory in 1904. This has a plaque to the Palmers and another to the **Heath and Hampstead Society**, who in 1994 raised funds to restore the structure, now a flower stall rather than a fountain.

College Crescent, just north of the Swiss Cottage, c. 1905. The New College is to the left of the picture.

John Constable

Inspired by the Heath's openness to the elements, where he could study the sky, Constable (1776-1837) occupied a succession of second homes in Hampstead. His first home in Hampstead was Albion Cottage, opposite **Whitestone Pond**, which he rented in 1819 the year he was grudgingly elected an Associate of the Royal Academy. He wrote in September 1820 to his friend Archdeacon Fisher "1 have

John Constable.

settled my wife and children comfortably at Hampstead. I am glad to get them out of London for every reason". He lived at No.2 Lower Terrace from 1821 until 1823, when he moved to Stamford Lodge on the eastern side of **Heath Street**. Three years later he moved to No.2 Langham Place, **Downshire Hill**, "a spot in a Valley just before you enter the town". The following year he moved to No.40 (then No.5) Well Walk, where he remained until 1834.

After he came to Hampstead, Constable painted fewer landscapes of his beloved Stour valley and turned to other places including Hampstead itself. He painted three views of Grove House (later **Admiral's House**) and a view of London with **Steele's Cottage** (*see p. 118*).

His wife Maria spent just one happy year in Well Walk before she died in 1828, and the success which at last came to Constable (in 1829 he was elected RA) seemed hollow to him. In 1833 he gave two lectures on the history of landscape painting at the Hampstead **Assembly Rooms**. In the same year he became a founder-member of Hampstead Public Library.

Maria and John Constable are buried in the same grave in the south-east corner of the churchyard of **St John's**, Hampstead.

The Dispensary

The Dispensary movement evolved in the later 18th century to provide poor people with medical treatment cheaply or free of charge to the recipient. The costs were normally paid by wealthier citizens who could nominate deserving cases for treatment. Highgate set up its dispensary in 1787. Hampstead was rather later on the scene. A sick relief club and self-supporting dispensary, formed by Rev. Thomas Ainger and other leading parishioners, began in 1846 with a small membership. This had risen to nearly 1,000 by 1851, when the name was changed to Hampstead Provident Dispensary.

The dispensary rented rooms in the New End **workhouse** until a three-storeyed building was built at

Resentful-looking donkeys being ridden on Hampstead Heath in 1859. Below, donkeys and their owner posing at Whitestone Pond c. 1905.

The proposed Dispensary and Soup Kitchen at New End. Drawing by its architect, R Hesketh.

No.16 New End and opened in 1853. The dispensary offered cheap medicine to the poor and shared premises with a soup kitchen that offered a pint of soup for a penny. A branch for West Hampstead was opened at No.33 Mill Lane before 1888. After the National Insurance Act, 1911, the dispensary gradually lost its importance and closed in 1948. The building at New End was converted into an architect's office in 1955.

Donkeys

Even before the fairs took over the Heath it had become a place for donkey rides. From the 1820s the Vestry had debated the nuisance of donkey touts and there were said to be 100 donkeys daily on the heath in 1836. Soon their popularity inspired cartoonists and attracted Charles Dickens and even, in the early 1850s, Karl Marx. When it took over the Heath in 1872 the Metropolitan Board of Works set up donkey stands near the **Vale of Health** and at the foot of **Downshire Hill**.

Downshire Hill, c.1930, looking towards St John's church. This watercolour by Mary Hill (1870-1947) is one of several reproduced in this book. Mary Hill is noted for her watercolours of Hampstead, a number of which were printed in postcard form and in her book Hampstead in Light and Shade.

Residents soon petitioned against Sunday rides and in 1873 the drivers' noisy plying for trade led to their being licensed and controlled. In 1876 concerns about the welfare of the donkeys contributed to the establishment of a Hampstead branch of the RSPCA. At the time Walford noted the troops of donkeys and donkey-boys who risked losing their licence should their onslaughts match "the torture to which the poor animals were subjected in bygone days".

George **du Maurier** nicknamed Whitestone Pond 'Ponds Asinorum' because of the many donkey stands there. A drinking trough was built for the donkeys standing at the foot of Downshire Hill. The donkeys were largely gone from the Heath before the First World War but some remained until the 1990s.

Downshire Hill Triangle

The Downshire Hill triangle, embracing Keats Grove and the upper part of South End Road, is one of the great pleasures of Hampstead. A satisfying number of the stuccoed brick Regency villas have survived. Many have stayed family houses and most are Listed buildings.

William Coleman, a Kentish developer, began building on a large area of copyhold land east of the London road in 1813. He was made bankrupt and his interest was conveyed in 1817 to William Woods, who designed and built **St John's Downshire Hill** and probably most of the houses on the estate. By 1830 a new, predominantly middle or lower middle class community had emerged. The

area remained unaltered until demolitions and extensions forty years later, when the streets between Flask Walk to the north and Pond Street to the south were laid out. It lost its cachet in the late 19th century, becoming working class in places but was gentrified again between the world wars, and is now very desirable.

The street name of Downshire Hill perhaps relates to the first Marquis of Downshire (1718-93), Secretary of State for the American colonies. The road has many associations with painters. For a short while **Constable** and his family were at Nos.25-26, then known as Langham Place. No.47 was home in the 1920s and 1930s to the painter Richard Carline (1896-1980), later a prime mover in the Hampstead Artists' Council. He belonged to a group of

Herbert Asquith, who lived at 12 Keats Grove, here caricatured in Vanity Fair.

modern painters including Stanley Spencer, Mark Gertler and Henry Lamb, sometimes called the Downshire Hill Group. Picasso's biographer, the art expert Roland Penrose (1900-84), lived at No.21 before World War Two and after it, joined by the photographer Lee Miller (1907-77).

The Freemason's Arms, first mentioned in the rate books of 1819, has been frequently rebuilt and was once famous for its pell mell court. The pub basement has, however, kept its old skittle alley which is the last of its kind in London. The pub has hosted a running club since the 1930s.

No.37 was Flora Robson's (1902-84) pre-war address after her success as Elizabeth I in *Fire over England* in 1936, while Dame Peggy Ashcroft (1907-91) lived after the war in one of the first blocks of flats in the area, Hampstead Hill Mansions. The flats were were on the site of Spring Cottage, where Dante Gabriel Rossetti (1828-82) and Lizzie Siddal lived after their marriage in 1860; Rossetti thought Hampstead "pretty well beyond civilization". No.49a was built by and for architects Sir Michael and Lady Patty Hopkins in 1975-76. Radically modern, the two-storey house is entirely glazed and barely noticeable from the road. The final building at the top of the street was **Hampstead Magistrates' Court**, closed in 1998.

Keats Grove was known until 1910 as John Street, but then renamed after its most famous resident. Adjoining **Keats House** is the Heath Branch Library, designed by Sydney Trent and opened in 1931 together with the Keats Memorial Library. Opposite, No.11A was the home (1973-83) of playwright Alan Ayckbourn. No.12 was the residence of future Prime Minister H H Asquith (1852-1928), who came here in 1877; ten years later his only daughter, the future Lady Violet Bonham-Carter (1887-1969), was born at the house. After moving from Greenhill,

Dame Edith Sitwell's (1887-1964) last days were spent at No.20. Sarah Coleridge and her children lived in the street; her father, the poet, when not too affected by laudanum, would stroll across the Heath from his home in Highgate to visit them.

Ducking Pool

Close to Richborough Road, in the north-west corner of Hampstead, was once a pool where it is said that in Anglo-Saxon times women would be ducked for "transgressing against the peace of their households and the credit of the community". However, there is a reference in a 10th-century charter to a 'cucking pool' in this corner of the monks' estate, which more probably acted as a cesspit. The punishment for scolds and others would be for them to be 'cucked' in dung.

Du Maurier Family

Three generations of this well-known family lived in Hampstead.

George du Maurier (1834-96) was born of Anglo-French parentage in Paris, where he studied painting and was friendly with Whistler. After he became blind in one eye he turned to book illustration. Moving to London he worked for *Punch* and developed his skill as a cartoonist, producing satires on the pretensions of high society and the affectations of the Aesthetic Movement. From 1869 he and his family were renting in Hampstead, and settled at No.27 **Church Row** in 1870, before moving to New Grove House in 1874. He began writing novels. In his most popular book, *Trilby*, the

George du Maurier; photograph by Elliot & Fry.

Gerald du Maurier in a scene with Marie Lohr in the 1920s.

musician Svengali mesmerizes a tone-deaf Irish model, Trilby O'Ferrall, who becomes a world-famous singer. It gave two expressions (Svengali, and the trilby hat) to the English language. Du Maurier moved in 1895 from Hampstead to Paddington, where he died the following year. Of surprise at the time, his body was cremated; the ashes were interred at St John's.

George had five children. The youngest, Gerald (1873-1934), was born in Church Row. He became an actor, serving his apprenticeship with Herbert Beerbohm Tree and then associated with J M Barrie, playing Hook in the first production of *Peter Pan* (1904). From 1910 to 1925, in partnership with Frank Curzon, Gerald du Maurier managed Wyndham's Theatre, after which he joined Gilbert Miller at the St James's Theatre to direct and star in many plays. He was one of the last great actor-managers.

Gerald lived from 1916 until his death in 1934 at **Cannon**

Hall and here Daphne du Maurier (1907-89), second of his three daughters, spent her childhood. She was educated mainly at home, and had a rather too close relationship with her father. He encouraged her to write stories and poetry and her fourth book *Gerald*, a frank biography written when he died in 1934, made her name. *Jamaica Inn* (1936) was an instant best-seller, as was *Rebecca* (1938). These and several other novels were made into films. Her short story *The Birds* became famous in the hands of Alfred Hitchcock in 1963. She died of heart failure at her home in Cornwall in 1989 and her ashes were scattered there.

East Heath Road

This twisting road alongside the Heath runs down from **Whitestone Pond** to South End. It was once known as Middle Heath Road, acquiring its present name in the 1860s. A century later it was

threatened with plans for a **Motorway Box** which would have turned the road into a Hampstead Village By-Pass, but the plans for this six-lane motorway were averted by the efforts of local protesters, headed by the **Heath and Hampstead Society** and the newly formed South End Green Association.

At the top of the hill, Bellmoor flats (1929) are named after the imposing residence originally on this site of **Thomas Barratt**. In the 1930s residents included Wimbledon champion Bunny Austin and conductor Sir Thomas Beecham.

No.22, Ladywell Court, is the remains of a mansion that was the home of the Holford family. The house was known as Heathfield in the 1870s, when the grounds were sold for building and the Hampstead Reformatory School for Girls moved here. No.17 bears a blue plaque to the writer Katherine Mansfield (1888-1923) and her husband Middleton Murry (1889-1957). Soon after their marriage in 1918 they moved into this grey-painted, tall house they nicknamed the Elephant.

In the autumn of 1920, when the Hampstead air had failed to cure her tuberculosis, she moved to Italy.

Katherine Mansfield.

Above, The Logs, an enormous pile in East Heath Road, at the corner with Well Road. Right is Klippan House at the corner of Well Walk and East Heath Road, designed by Ewan Christian.

On the corner of Well Road stands the forbidding Victorian pile called The Logs, completed in 1868. In 1951 the house was converted into maisonettes, one of which was occupied in the late 1960s by comedian Marty Feldman (1934-82).

There is fortunately little building on the Heath side apart from two large Edwardian blocks of flats, The Pryors (1908). Opposite, controversial philo-sopher Cyril Joad (1891-1953) lived for many years at No.4, which he found "ugly but comfortable". In the 1930s he championed mixed hockey on the Heath which had been banned until then. In the same decade Sir Arthur Bliss lived in the nearby,

creeper-covered East Heath Lodge, which turns the corner into Heath Side, with its delightful 18th-century houses.

Electricity Supply

In 1891 several companies were competing to be allowed to supply electric light to Hampstead residents, but the Vestry decided that it would supply them itself and formed

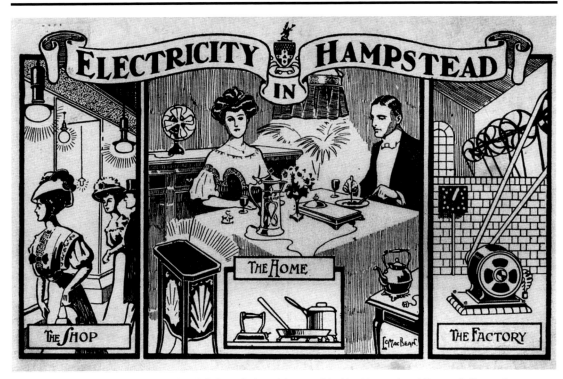

A postcard advertising the delights of electricity provided by Hampstead Borough Council.

its own electricity undertaking. It was only the second local authority, after St Pancras, to do so. A decade earlier it had bought a piece of land between the railways in West Hampstead, which it had been using as a stone yard: hence the name of the street there, Lithos Road. Its Central Supply Station was erected in the stoneyard at a cost of just over £9,000 and the electricity supply commenced on 1 October 1894, using a high tension system. This gave a good reach but had to be kept in constant service, requiring ten tons of coal a day. Locals complained about the 140 ft-chimney belching out coal fumes.

The initial number of customers was 246, which had risen to more than 8,000 by 1914. By then the local authority had committed over £500,000 towards expenditure on its electricity supply system. There was very little profit, but consumers had a cheap and efficient supply and from 1909 Hampstead had converted street lights from gas to electricity.

Bulk supply from St Marylebone commenced in April 1921 and the Lithos Road station ceased to generate in 1922. It was subsequently used as offices until 1983 when housing was built on the site.

England's Lane

Shown on Rocque's map of 1745, England's Lane started life as the pathway that led to Upper **Chalcots** Farm, which appeared in records in 1253. The farm was leased in 1776 to James England, hence the road's present name. By 1870 building had begun at the west end of the Lane, where the Washington public house, was named after the birthplace in Sussex of the busy developer, Daniel Tidey. He also built the local shops. Chalcot Gardens, a narrow roadway fronting England's Lane includes a striking Arts and Crafts house at No.16, once home to the illustrator Arthur Rackham (1867-1939).

Eton College Estate

The College in 1826 obtained an Act to grant 99-year building leases. In 1830 **Adelaide Road** was begun and a small-scale builder, William Wynn, built houses fronting Haverstock Hill. Builders were however held back by the prospect of the London & Birmingham Railway. It was not until 1839 that development really got underway, and it was piecemeal as the College

England's Lane c.1905, looking towards Belsize Park Gardens.

rejected an overall plan for the estate. It left responsibility for roads and sewers to its lessees.

Adelaide Road saw the earliest houses. King Henry's Road, which ran south of and parallel to it was laid out later with semi-detached Italianate villas. Apart from the small enclave around Eton Villas, begun in the 1840s, the roads immediately to the north of Adelaide Road were developed from the 1860s, as a residential area, with substantial houses on tree-lined streets like Eton Road and particularly imposing detached houses on broad Eton Avenue.

Steele's Cottage on Haverstock Hill was demolished in 1867 and replaced by a "very respectable row of shops" and by the new Steele's Road, lined with houses by the late 1870s. By then most of the north part of the estate was largely complete, except to the west where William Willett the elder (1837-1913) built red-brick houses in the 1880s and 1890s. The central portion of Eton Avenue was built in the first years of the 20th century.

To the south of Adelaide Road, the Willetts, father and son, linked the estate to **Avenue Road** by extending Elsworthy Road. This area, within easy reach of public transport, was and remains highly sought after. Its generous layout, with wide pavements, plane trees and privet hedges, was admired by Sir Raymond Unwin the designer of Hampstead Garden Suburb, who acknowledged his debt to William Willett Jr (1856-1915). The latter was a fanatical early riser, and an untiring advocate of Daylight Saving and Summer Time, introduced the year after his death in 1915. The future Edward VIII was a frequent visitor to No.48 in the early 1930s when he had an affair with Viscountess Furness, before she introduced him to her friend, Mrs Wallis Simpson. The invigorating conductor Sir Georg Solti (1912-97) lived for many years at No.51, while No.4 was home from 1905 to 1937 to the conductor Sir Henry Wood, famous for his direction of the Proms. His house was much visited by Richard Strauss and other composers. At nearby No.32 Elsworthy Road, the home in the 1990s of rock star Liam Gallagher and actress Patsy Kensit was frequently door-stepped by the paparazzi.

By 1913 building was complete throughout the Eton College estate but after the First World War large houses tended to be converted to flats and in the 1930s, when the first leases began to fall in, the earliest villas in their long gardens were replaced by large blocks of flats, as happened elsewhere in the borough.

The estate was badly damaged during the Second World War. The council redeveloped certain areas from the 1950s. In 1954 it began work on the Fellows Road Estate, not

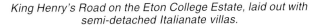

King Henry's Road on the Eton College Estate, laid out with semi-detached Italianate villas.

33

finally completed until 1976, which became part of the large Chalcots Estate, centred on Adelaide Road. Begun in 1965 this featured high-rise concrete blocks named after places near Eton. Elsewhere, a good deal of the original stuccoed, semi-detached villas remain, many Listed. This includes all of the 'Italian rustic' houses in Eton Villas, where the architect of the National Portrait Gallery, Ewan Christian (1814-95), lived at No.6 in the 1850s and the architectural historian Sir John Summerson (1904-92) resided until his death in 1992 at No.1, and the pastel-painted houses in adjoining Provost Road.

The Everyman

The Everyman building was opened in 1888 as the Holly Bush Vale drill hall for the **Hampstead Rifle Volunteers**. After World War One the windows were blocked up and in 1920 it opened as a theatre, with a steeply raked floor and seating for 300. It was run by Norman MacDermott (1890-1977), who with the encouragement of Bernard Shaw and John Galsworthy made it a home of intelligent and experimental drama. Many famous players including Mrs Patrick Campbell, Dame Edith Evans and Ellen Terry, appeared here. Noel Coward's then shocking play *The Vortex*, about drug addiction among the upper classes, opened here in 1924 before achieving huge success on the West End stage.

MacDermott was however always short of money: the building work had been expensive and Hampstead's residents did not provide many of the bookings. New partners took control in 1926.

In 1933 James Fairfax-Jones

A production of the play Low Tide *at the Everyman in 1924. The actor Claude Rains is on the right, looking down at Olive Sloane.*

converted the Everyman into a cinema and he and his family ran it for the next fifty years. It is no longer London's leading venue for art house films; a change in ownership in the 1990s led to its conversion to more mainstream cinema.

Fairs

The first recorded fair in Hampstead was held in the early 18th century in **Flask Walk**. In 1712, this was an annual event, lasting four days. It was noted for its riotous character, akin to the Smithfield Fair. It had closed by mid century and may have transferred to Hampstead's **West End**.

The origins of the West End fair are, however, unknown. By the late 18th century there was a small three-day toy and gingerbread fair in high summer, with booths furnished by Hampstead ladies. It was celebrated in 1802 by Mrs Barbauld as the fair "where Charity with Fashion meets". The fair was nevertheless associated with the local Cock and Hoop pub and soon began to attract unsavoury elements from London, or so local

property owners feared. Following a public meeting, the fair was presented in 1812 as a great nuisance and the Lady of the Manor issued instructions that she would not permit the fair at West End or anywhere else. Local tradesmen foiled the first attempts at suppression and the fair became even larger, with shows trading on the physical deformity of the human and animal exhibits, attracting big crowds. In 1815, for example, Gyngell included Dutch-born Mr Paap, "the smallest man in the world" at 28 inches high. In 1819, when the fair expanded into a field in Mill Lane, some 200 ruffians broke up the booths, overwhelmed the local constables, and committed violent robbery, for which at least three of them were later hanged. The local West End magistrate Germain Lavie, supported by the manorial court, the Vestry, and a separate committee, promoted a military-style operation in 1820 in which 150 police and special constables were deployed to prevent the fair taking place. Thereafter, no attempts were made to revive it.

The fairs for which

A fair on Hampstead Heath, early 20th century.

Hampstead is most famous have taken place on the Heath. These seem to have begun there in the early 19th century, possibly linked to the suppression of the West End fair. After the opening of **Hampstead Heath station** in 1860 and especially after the Bank Holiday Act of 1871, which enforced four extra one-day holidays in a year, large-scale fairs were provided to cater for the London crowds. Booths on the Heath were recorded from about 1865, steam merry-go-rounds and swings appeared by Easter 1878, and the following Easter saw a fair at **South End Green**, while swings and other entertainments were provided at the **Vale of Health** and on East Heath by the 1880s. Fairs on the Heath have remained popular ever since. See **'Appy 'Ampstead**.

Famous Names

Hampstead has attracted so many famous names that a separate publication would be needed to list them all. Recommended is the **Hampstead Museum's** booklet *Where They Lived in Hampstead*. It features a cartoon of a disconsolate American tourist reading a plaque announcing "The Only House in Hampstead That Nobody Famous Lived In".

Recorded below is a selection of those not mentioned elsewhere in this book.

No.1 and No.3 Lyndhurst Terrace, were built in 1864 for two brothers-in-law, both stained-glass artists: Alfred Bell, co-founder of Clayton & Bell, and John Burlison, co-founder of Burlison & Grylls. The artist and art critic Roger Fry (1866-1934) lived at No.22 Willow Road from 1903, Duncan Grant (1885-1978) was at No.143 Fellows Road around 1910, while the much

more traditional painter Sir Frank Dicksee (1853-1828) was based at No.3 Greville Place for many years. In the 1930s the Vorticist painter David Bomberg (1890-1987) lived at No.10 Fordwych Road, before moving to other Hampstead addresses, while Charles Ginner (1878-1952), one of the founders of the Camden Town Group, lived at No.61 High Street in the mid 1930s. He painted several views down Flask Walk (*see back cover*). At the same period, the cartoonist David Low (1891-1963), creator of Colonel Blimp, had a studio at No.13A Heath Street. No.3 Eldon Grove was the home of the painter Paul Nash (1889-1944). The artist Mary Hill (1870-1947), famous for her postcard views of Hampstead, lived at No.8 Thurlow Road.

In the same house (from 1954) lived the Bulgarian author Elias Canetti, who won the Nobel Prize for Literature in 1981. He wrote a sensational memoir of his Hampstead

Gladys Cooper, who lived in Elsworthy Road.

Thompson (1929-82) creator of the *Magic Roundabout* and father of the actress Emma.

Among other actors are Anna Neagle (1904-86), at No.14 Holly Hill in the late 1930s, when Gladys Cooper (1888-1971) was at No.35 Elsworthy Road. In the early 1950s Richard Burton could be found rehearsing Shakespeare on the lawn of No.6 Lyndhurst Road and soon after Manor Lodge in Frognal Lane became home to Peggy Ashcroft (1907-91). At No.69 Frognal the actor and film star Anton Walbrook died in 1967, and No.8 Frognal Gardens was home to Alastair Sim (1900-76).

Hampstead has had a strong poetic tradition ever since Leigh Hunt moved here. Recent poets have included Geoffrey Grigson (1905-85) and Louis Macneice (1907-63) who in turn made No.4A Keats Grove their home, and John Drinkwater (1882-1937) at North Hall, Mortimer Crescent, from 1934 until his death in 1937.

Publishers, long attracted to Hampstead, included Sir Geoffrey Faber (1889-1961) at No.1 Oak Hill Park in the 1930s and 1940s and Sir Stanley Unwin (1884-1968), who lived opposite him from the 1930s and formed a company to buy the war-damaged Victorian houses in Oak Hill Park from the Neave family; he failed, and built No.4 for himself.

Melanie Klein, the Viennese-born psychoanalyst, lived her last years in the 1950s at No.16 Bracknell Gardens.

Two politicians not otherwise mentioned are Anthony Greenwood (1911-82), Baron Greenwood of Rossendale, who lived at No.38 Downshire Hill and Baroness Serota of Hampstead. She had a distinguished political career

John Drinkwater, resident in Mortimer Crescent, in 1923. Drawing by Walter Tittle.

and died in 2002 at her home of many years, No.15 Lynd-hurst Terrace. Her son, Nicholas, is Director of Tate Modern.

Frances Buss (1827-94), the educationalist, lived at Myra Lodge at the corner of King Henry's Road and Primrose Hill Road from 1868.

Graham Hill (1929-75), the racing driver, lived at No.63 Glenmore Road after the war, and his son Damon, also a Formula One World Champ-ion, was born there in 1960.

Fascism

There were regular fascist meetings at **Whitestone Pond** in the 1930s. After his release from prison in 1946, Oswald Mosley revisited Hampstead in 1946 to address a 'literary discussion' in Prince Arthur Road. He formed a new political party, the Union Movement, which had a Hampstead branch, spurred on by some antipathy to the very large number of Jewish refugees

days, *Party in the Blitz* (2005), which included his assignations with the then unknown author Iris Murdoch – at No.8. Other writers associated with Hampstead have included Robert Louis Stevenson (1850-94) who lodged in Abernethy House, Mount Vernon, several times in the late 19th century. He wrote to a friend in Scotland that the air was surprisingly good. Antrim Mansions in Antrim Road was home to Frank Richards (1876-1961) (real name Charles Hamilton), creator of *Billy Bunter*; he lived here 1908-11. Evelyn Waugh (1903-66) was born at Dunedin, No.11 Hillfield Road. Mary Webb (1881-1927) was at No.12 Hampstead Grove from 1923. No.28 Lymington Road was then the home of Edmund Clerihew Bentley (1875-1956), writer of detective novels and who gave his middle name to a literary form. The playwright Alan Ayckbourn was born at No.32 Glenloch Road. No.30 Crediton Hill was the home from 1970 until 1982 of Eric

Fenton House c.1898, a lithograph by Thomas Way.

in the area after the war. An 'anti-alien' petition had been launched in the borough in October 1945 that, under the pretext of securing homes for returning ex-servicemen, campaigned for the removal of the district's predominantly Jewish refugee population. The Union Movement's first meeting in Hampstead was at Whitestone Pond but this and further open-air meetings were regularly disrupted. The Union Movement's candidate polled only 81 votes in the local elections in 1949, and the movement faded away.

Fenton House

The oldest surviving mansion in Hampstead, usually said to have been built in 1693 (a date found on a chimney) although the National Trust, its present owners, now think a local bricklayer erected it seven years earlier. In 1706, as Ostend House, it was sold to Joshua Gee, a Quaker silk merchant with business dealings in America, who was one of the mortgagees of Pennsylvania

and author of a protectionist tract on trade. In 1793 the property, then known as The Clock House after a clock-face on its façade, was bought by Philip Fenton, a Riga merchant. He left it to his nephew, James, who added the loggia and new entrance on the east side.

Barratt says Queen Victoria visited Fenton House when it was let to her lady-in-waiting Lady Abercrombie but there is no evidence the latter was here. The last private owner, Lady Binning, who died in 1952, left the house and its splendid walled garden to the National Trust. It houses the unique Benton-Fletcher collection of early keyboard instruments, including a 1612 harpsichord once used by Handel. Visiting students are permitted to play the instruments, but the house should also be seen for its pictures, porcelain and furniture.

Finchley Road

This was constructed as a turnpike road by Colonel Henry Samuel Eyre, to increase

the development value of the St John's Wood estate which he owned. It was to prove a costly investment and he had to contend with opposition.

Sir Thomas Maryon Wilson, Lord of Hampstead Manor, had different ideas. He saw that Eyre's plan was entirely self-interested and felt that Hampstead's "quiet and privacy will be disturbed and diminished". He thwarted Eyre's first three attempts at obtaining an Act of Parliament, but this was finally passed in 1826. However, work went ahead very slowly. There were problems raising funds and the surveyor was incompetent and was dismissed, after trying to excuse himself by saying he had accidentally and fatally poisoned his wife!

The road opened in 1830 (as Finchley New Road) but the returns were poor and never approached the £3,000 stated in the prospectus. After ten years without any interest payment or return on his capital one of the investors, Captain Randall, seized the road in 1840 and himself let the tolls, as he was legally entitled to do. He disbursed the tolls for his and other investors' benefit and told trustees to apply to parishes to maintain the road. Responsibility for the turnpike was later given to the Metropolis Road Commission who retained the toll gates until 1871 when all debt had finally been repaid.

Finchley Road was initially seen as an expensive way of travelling nowhere in particular, and for decades there was little traffic. Indeed, a horse patrol was needed to protect early travellers from robbers because of its remoteness. While it helped stimulate development on

Finchley Road c. 1905.

Eyre's estate it was not until the 1880s that there was significant building activity between Swiss Cottage and Child's Hill. When the first of three local stations along the road, Finchley Road and Frognal, opened in 1860 it was in the middle of open country. It was followed in 1868 by the Midland Railway's Finchley Road station, built after the construction of the Belsize tunnel, a remarkable engineering feat. The station closed for passenger traffic in 1927 and now the O$_2$ shopping centre covers the site.

Housing spread northwards along the road in the 1880s and was virtually complete by 1913. This includes mansion flats and shops, many built by Edward Cave's firm. Baines noted that it had been newly planted with trees in 1889 and felt that "it promises to be the most imposing avenue or public highway near London".

But despite the presence from 1900 of John Barnes' department store (*see* **Shops**), it never became a major shopping street, and was fume-laden and dirty after traffic widening in the late 1960s turned it into a six-lane highway.

By then, most of the original houses had disappeared. The southern stretches of Finchley Road were totally rebuilt after World War Two. To the north, below West End Lane, Ednam House and studio was built in 1878-79 for the sculptor James Forsyth. A crane capable of lifting 20 tons was built in the yard because he specialised in large monumental works, such as the Perseus and Andromeda fountain at Witley Court, Worcestershire, described in 1862 as the largest piece of sculpture in Europe.

Above West End Lane, are mansion blocks such as Mandeville Court which was

briefly the refuge of the artist, Oskar Kokoschka, soon after fleeing from Austria in 1938. The imposing building at No.527 was built in 1887 for the Hackney Theological College for dissenting divinity students, which united with the New College in College Crescent in 1924. The building became known as Parsifal College. The college left in 1977 and the premises immediately became the London Regional Centre of the Open University. In 2004 No.527 became the UK campus of the ESCP-EAP international school of management that had originated in a commercial school founded in Paris in 1819. Next door No.527A, built as the West Hampstead Congregational Church by Spalding and Cross in 1894, was sold to the Shomrei Hadath Synagogue in 1946 who moved around the corner,

Hampstead Fire Station in Heath Street, c. 1905, opposite the site of today's Underground station.

when the building was developed into luxury flats called The Octagon in 1991.

Fire Stations

The Vestry had done little about fire-fighting other than supply a rather primitive pump-engine, so before the 1850s many houses relied on the fire brigades organised by rival fire insurers. The Metropolitan Fire Brigade, formed in 1856, opened its first station on **Haverstock Hill**, near the George. Four years later it transferred to a grand neo-Gothic building at the corner of **Heath Street** and Holly Hill, designed by the architect G Vulliamy.

The tower was also a water tower, a new development for London's horse-drawn fire brigade. Stables for horses were on the ground floor and there were mechanical devices for lowering saddles onto their backs. Originally taller than it is now, the tower was a useful observation post in World War One, though a warning rocket was fired which unfortunately did some damage to the nearby

Hampstead Parochial School. The station was closed in 1923 (the building survives with a shortened tower) but by then a new one was open in Lancaster Grove, designed by C C Winmill and now Listed. A branch station had already been built in 1901 in West End Lane.

The first motorized fire engines were not introduced until 1906, and horse-drawn carriages for fire engines continued in use until 1921.

Fitzjohn's Avenue

A grand boulevard laid out by the Maryon Wilson family after it was finally able to break the entail that had prevented building development. The loss of rich agricultural land caused an outcry from conservationists, notably from Octavia Hill, but in 1875 the fifty acres of land were sold to developers for £50,000 and the avenue was named after a Maryon Wilson estate in Essex. At first, from the Swiss Cottage end, it reached only as far as the new Arkwright Road. Beyond lay the tangle of old and congested courts near the parish church, but in the 1880s these were swept away and the Avenue was extended to join the redeveloped Heath Street.

Fitzjohn's Avenue was an immediate success, often compared with developments in Paris. In 1883 The American magazine *Harpers* gushed that it was "one of the noblest streets in the world". The Maryon Wilsons insisted in every building contract that no house "shall at any time be erected on the said piece of land of less value than £3,000", and the resultant houses were

Fitzjohn Tower in Fitzjohn's Avenue, designed by J T Wimperis, 1880-81.

The Three Gables at 6 Fitzjohn's Avenue, 1889, built for the artist Frank Holl.

suitably king-sized.

The architect Richard Norman Shaw (1831-1912), who designed his own house at No.6 Ellerdale Road near the top of the Avenue, was commissioned to build No.61 for the fashionable painter Edwin Long (1829-91) and also Three Gables (No.6) for the portrait painter Frank Holl (1845-88). Such popular artists soon dominated the avenue, and when their houses were opened on 'Show Sunday' they attracted the smart set from all over London. It inspired Bernard Shaw to make a character in *Mrs Warren's Profession* claim that she learned about art from "some artistic people in Fitzjohn's Avenue".

Its early inhabitants also included Lloyds underwriters, ship-owners, auctioneers and silk manufacturers. At the foot of the hill No.1 was home to Frank Debenham (1837-1917), the store owner, who died there. Later residents included the film director John Schlesinger (1926-2003) born at No.15 and the novelist Stella

Gibbons (1902-89) who had a bed-sit at No.67 in the early 1930s when writing her classic *Cold Comfort Farm*.

Wide streets parallel to Fitzjohn's Avenue were laid out. To the east, Daleham Gardens was fully developed by 1885 by H & E Kelly, who also built much of Fitzjohn's Avenue itself. No.22 was during the 1930s a boarding house run largely for Jewish refugees by Sybil Knight; she and her family often appeared in famous pictures made by one of her lodgers, the noted photographer Bill Brandt (1904-83). Daleham Mews was developed at the same time as the Gardens, primarily to provide stabling for the local residents. The actor, Roy Kinnear, lived at No.33 in the 1960s.

To the west Netherhall Gardens was given its present name in 1877 and became a prestigious address. In 1888 a second house was designed for Edwin Long by Richard Norman Shaw at No.42, Kelston, which was renamed Severn House when Elgar (1857-1934) moved in. No.51 bears a blue plaque to John Passmore Edwards (1823-1911), hailing him as "Builder of Free Public Libraries", but he also spent much of the money he made from publishing on hospitals and horse troughs. After their marriage in 1892, a flat at No.10 was the first home of social reformers and historians Sidney (1859-1947) and Beatrice Webb (1858-1943). In neighbouring Maresfield Gardens, **South Hampstead High School** was opened at the southern end in 1882 and Herbert Henry Asquith (1852-1928), then an MP, lived at No.27 from 1887 to 1892. Building on the area of the

former demesne land was complete by 1891, when it was solidly middle-class and wealthy, and so it has remained.

Flask Walk

Flask Walk starts as a narrow turning off the High Street, once arched over, but widens beyond the paved shopping parade and the Flask pub into a quiet residential street of spruced-up artisans' cottages. The present Flask dates only from 1874 but the original Lower Flask Tavern, which gave this old street its name, was the place where Spa water was once bottled for sale in the City. In Samuel Richardson's 1748 novel *Clarissa*, the Lower Flask was described as "a place where second-rate persons are to be found occasionally in a swinish condition".

Along the street is the nucleus of a village green, which was large enough in the early 18th century to hold Hampstead's first recorded fair. More permanently on the green were the village stocks and the watchman's hut, complete with

Flask Walk, looking west in the 1930s, watercolour by Mary Hill.

The entrance to Flask Walk off the High Street.
Drawing by A R Quinton c.1901.

Fleet Road

This busy road is on the line of an ancient footpath alongside the Fleet river linking **South End Green** with Gospel Oak. The land was considered too low-lying, ill-drained and unhealthy to be fit for middle-class housing, and its reputation further suffered with the arrival of the Midland Railway in 1868 and particularly with the fever hospital hastily erected in 1870 near **Hampstead Green**. Then in 1887 came the trams, with a large depot and stables built here. The Vestry ensured that trams did not penetrate any further into the town. Tramway history was made here in 1901, when the loop line along Constantine Road was created to avoid trams backing down Fleet Road. It was one of the first examples of one-way-street working, and the last stretch of tramway built for horse trams. Horses gave way to electricity in 1909. Many tram workers settled in the neighbourhood, and the area around Fleet Road became a working-class quarter.

two overnight cells. The Bath House at the Well Walk end, erected by the **Wells and Campden Trust**, has been converted into town houses (one called the Washhouse). Boade's Mews is both a passage and a house; Boade's Corner was the old name for this area. Nearby is Rose Mount on the corner of New End Square. It is adjacent to Rose Lodge. Alfred, Lord Tenny-

son's mother lived in the first, his sister in the second. Opposite Rose Mount is a wall containing a studded door that used to be the Debtors' Entrance to the infamous Newgate Gaol.

On the corner of Gardnor Road, a cul-de-sac off Flask Walk, is Gardnor House (1737) named after an 18th-century landowner who lived in it; it was home to Kingsley Amis (1922-95) in the 1980s.

Fortune Green

First recorded in 1646, The derivation of the name is uncertain. It is located where the old Blind Lane (now gone) met the road from West End to Cow House Farm in Hendon, a route which now bisects **Hampstead Cemetery** but still links up with Farm Avenue in Hendon.

Fortune Green was a four-acre patch of manorial waste where local residents had the right to graze animals, dig turf and play sports. There were regular cricket matches. In the 19th century the Lord of the

The old Wells and Campden Trust baths in Flask Walk, now converted into apartments.

Gipsies encamped on Fortune Green, c. 1887.

Manor granted enclosure rights for about a third of the area and nine cottages were built here from 1820, housing labourers and laundresses, who were allowed to keep drying poles on the Green for fourpence a year.

In 1875, more of the open space was lost to the new Hampstead Cemetery and in the 1880s the whole area was threatened with redevelopment, after two copyholders had become enfranchised. A Fortune Green Protection Society was formed in July 1891 and a month later held its first large meeting on the Green. The Green was then home to many gipsies, who refused to leave; in December the crowd pulled their caravans off and the Vestry had fifty posts put up. The two freeholders issued a writ of trespass against the Vestry, who in the ensuing court case pleaded the right of recreation on the Green. The judge ruled that there was insufficient evidence to show Fortune Green was a village green and the Vestry was ordered to pay costs. It decided to buy the land from the freeholders. £8,000 had to be raised. Most of the purchase price was met by the Vestry with help from the LCC; £1,647 was collected by public subscription, over half of which came, as usual, from **Sir Henry Harben**. So the Green became public land in 1897, and at the start of 1898 was turfed and paths laid out.

Today the Green offers a fenced-off Play Centre for children and every July is used in the local Jester on the Green Festival. Next to the Green a large new development of luxury flats by Piers Gough of CZWG architects was under construction in 2009.

Sigmund Freud

The psychoanalyst Sigmund Freud (1856-1939) fled Vienna and Nazi persecution in 1938. He was aged 82, with no money and suffering from cancer. After a brief stay at No.59 Elsworthy Road he moved to No.20 Maresfield Gardens where he charged patients between three and five guineas for an hour's therapy. Freud was visited by Salvador Dali and by H G Wells and completed the book *Moses and Monotheism*, in which he argued Moses was not Jewish but Egyptian. He died the following year, but his daughter Anna, a children's psychoanalyst, who opened a clinic in the house in 1952, maintained his rooms intact until her death thirty years later. The house was opened as the Freud Museum in 1986. Visitors can see the library and study, which contain the great

Sigmund Freud, who spent his last year in Maresfield Gardens.

The writer and illustrator, Kate Greenaway, in her studio. Her house at 39 Frognal was designed by R Norman Shaw.

man's personal collection of antiquities and books, as well as his psychoanalytic couch. A bronze statue of Freud by Oscar Nemon, designed in Vienna in 1930, was erected in Fitzjohn's Avenue at the junction with Belsize Lane in 1997.

Frognal

A name which denotes an area, but it is also a charming and leafy street meandering between Hampstead and West Hampstead. Frognal was the site of the first settlement in the parish, huddling around the Frognal Brook and a sprinkling of village ponds. The ancient name means 'the place of frogs', who must have thrived in this once watery area. Up until the 19th century there was a scatter of buildings at the junction of Frognal and Frognal Lane which belonged to the Lord and, in particular, to his Manor Farm, also known as Hall Oak Farm. This was the absentee Lord's headquarters and his bailiff's office but it was not the Manor House: there wasn't one.

Frognal was recorded in the early 15th century as a 'customary tenement', an estate held on condition that the customs of the manor of Hampstead were adhered to. The original house was probably on the site of No.99 Frognal (otherwise called Frognal House), which dates from about 1740. In World War Two it became the home (1940-42) of General de Gaulle, self-styled leader of the Free French. At this time Winston Churchill referred to De Gaulle as "the monster of Hampstead". The house was bought by the Sisters of St Dorothy in 1968 as an international finishing school for girls.

During the 17th and 18th centuries Frognal gained a reputation for the "salubrity of its air and soil" and grew into a collection of cottages and mansions, many of which adopted the Frognal name. Its exclusive air was destroyed by the Finchley Road being pushed through the demesne land to the west, although development was delayed until the 1870s, by when Oak Hill Park, a new road running west from Frognal had been built. In 1851 this had won a Great Exhibition Award for Gentlemen's Dwellings. George Smith (1824-1901), founder of the *Dictionary of National Biography*, lived from 1863 to 1872 in Oak Hill Lodge, where he entertained leading writers and artists. Florence Nightingale was a frequent visitor to Oak Hill Park, where Manley Hopkins, an authority on maritime law, lived in the 1850s with his family, including Gerard, the future poet. Michael Lyell's design in the early 1960s of five seven-storeyed blocks of luxury flats on the Oak Hill Park Estate, which replaced the 19th-century houses, won a Civic Trust award.

The demesne land to the west of Oak Hill was laid out with new roads from the mid 1870s, notably Redington Road, which curved from Frognal to West Heath. In 1876 Nos.2 and 4, "a wonderfully subtle pair", were designed by Philip Webb. Building thereafter was slow; No.16 (One Oak) designed by A H Mackmurdo in 1889 was later home to the sculptor Sir Hamo Thornycroft (1850-1925), then to the civil engineer Sir Owen Williams (1890-1969) and in the 1970s to actors John Alderton and Pauline Collins. Another star of *Upstairs, Downstairs*, Gordon Jackson (1923-90), lived at No.36, and master showman Lord Bernard Delfont (1909-94) lived at No.42A. On the opposite side, Nos.35-37, Redington Lodge, was home in the late 1930s of LSE sociologist Professor Morris Ginsberg (1889-1970).

The old road, Frognal, had been extended southward beyond Arkwright Road by 1878 and reached Finchley Road soon afterwards. The architect Basil Champneys (1842-1935) built himself a house (No.42 Frognal Lane) on the site of Manor Farm. At the height of her fame as a children's book illustrator, Kate Greenaway (1846-1901) commissioned the fashionable and local Norman Shaw to design her a tile-hung studio house at No.39 Frognal in 1885. She died there in 1901 but her name lives on in nearby Greenaway Gardens. The poet Stephen Spender (1909-95) grew up at No.10.

In the 1930s houses were built on the east side of Frognal. In 1938 the provocative design of No.66 by Connell, Ward & Lucas, pioneers of the Modern Movement, caused a local furore, but is now hailed as the best pre-war modern house in England, Listed Grade II*. It fulfils all of Le Corbusier's five points of architecture.

Frognal still contains several 18th-century houses and is well worth a walk. The first Labour premier, Ramsay Macdonald (1866-1937) lived at No.103 from 1925-37; his residence here was much criticised by socialists. Nearby, the contralto Kathleen Ferrier (1912-53) has a plaque on 97 Frognal Mansions, where she lived from 1942 until her death in 1953.

Frognal Grove

Now divided up into Nos.103-109 Frognal, this house was built by the architect Henry Flitcroft about 1745, replacing an earlier property. In the later 18th century Frognal Grove was occupied by an eminent lawyer, Edward Montagu, a leader of the **Philo-Investigists**. After his death, the house was renamed in his honour and it was enlarged by the architect G E Street in the 1860s.

Frognal Hall

Adjoining the parish church-yard once stood Frognal Hall which probably existed by 1646. It became the residence of Isaac Ware (c.1704-66), who aided by Lord Burlington, raised himself from a humble chimney-sweep to eminent architect. He was the author of a translation of Palladio's *Architecture*. By 1791 the house was the home of Sir Richard Pepper Arden (1744-1804), Master of the Rolls, later Lord Alvanley and Lord Chief Justice of the Common Pleas. His small stature, clothed in long robes, made him the butt of caricaturists. The Hall survived until the 1920s as did the neighbouring Priory Lodge, where according to Boswell Dr Johnson lodged his wife for the country air and where on one visit he wrote most of the *Vanity of Human Wishes*. "One man can learn more in a journey by the Hampstead coach", Johnson opined, "than another can in making the grand tour of Europe".

Frognal (Old) Mansion

This rather grave, two-storeyed building at No.94 Frognal stands at right angles to the street. The centre part dates from about 1700. Up till the later 19th century, part of the manorial rights attached to this property was a private toll-gate on the adjoining lane leading up to the church. A toll of one penny for each cart or carriage was exacted. The Vestry eventually had the toll-gate removed having recompensed the owner, Alexander Gray who bought the Old Mansion in about 1889. He commissioned James Neale, a former pupil of G E Street, to add a wing to the old house.

Through the grounds, Gray laid out an L-shaped road, Frognal Gardens, where Neale designed five houses, including No.18 (Frognal End), built in 1892 for the novelist and antiquary Sir Walter Besant (1836-1901). It was the home from the 1940s of Labour leader Hugh Gaitskell (1906-63), who when Chancellor of the Exchequer in 1950, even rejected No.11 Downing Street in favour of No.18 Frognal Gardens.

Frognal Priory

John 'Memory' Thompson, an eccentric who made a fortune as a public house auctioneer, created Frognal Priory, a pastiche mansion of many styles, in about 1820. Thompson boasted he had a better memory than any man

Old Frognal Priory in 1830.

inhabitant of the 'priory'. People flocked from far and near to see it. After his death, his niece and her husband did not pay the customary fine to the Lord of the Manor, and Sir Thomas Maryon Wilson recovered possession by an injunction. But the house was left to moulder and in 1876 it was pulled down.

It was to be replaced by another remarkable house of the same name designed by Norman Shaw. He was commissioned in 1885 by Edwin Tate, an executive of sugar refiners Tate & Lyle. Demolished in the 1930s, the group of modernist houses called Frognal Close was built on its site by **Sigmund Freud**'s son.

living and offered to prove it by stating the name and business of every person who kept a corner shop in the City. Thompson asserted (without foundation) that he had built his house on the site of an ancient priory. As an auctioneer, he had the opportunity of collecting old furniture and pieces of carving in exotic woods and ivory, etc. which he said belonged to Cardinal Wolsey, a former

A principal sitting room at New Frognal Priory in 1885, designed by R Norman Shaw.

The sculptor Gilbert Bayes (1872-1953) at work in his studio in Greville Place. His best known work is the ornamental clock outside Selfridge's.

Frognal Way

Described as the "showpiece of interwar Hampstead housing" this unadopted, wide cul-de-sac was laid out in 1924 over Priory Lodge. Maxwell Fry's Sun House of 1935-36 at No.9 was the first modernist concrete house within the built-up area of London, now Listed Grade II*. At No.20 is Mediterranean-style Blue Tiles, designed by R L Page in 1934 for Gracie Fields (1898-1979) and her first husband, Archie Pitt.

Golders Hill Park

All but its southern extremity lies outside Hampstead. It was possibly Charles Dingley (d. 1769) who created the Golders Hill estate in the 18th century. He built the large house there. Dingley was persuaded by the Government to stand against John Wilkes in the Middlesex elections, but was attacked by a Wilkite mob and died. Repton later landscaped the grounds.

The last owner of Golders Hill was Spencer Wells, surgeon to Queen Victoria. He died in 1897 and the estate was put up for sale. A committee made up of local grandees agreed to bid up to £35,000, but **Thomas Barratt** secured it for £38,000 and then conveyed his contract to the committee, which recouped its expenses after a public appeal. This raised £41,000, with the LCC giving £12,000 and Hampstead Vestry £10,000.

The LCC took over the property, which opened as a public park in December 1898. The house was used as a refreshment room but was demolished by a landmine in 1941, and there is now another café on the site. The park is today managed by the City of London as part of Hampstead Heath

Golders Hill House at North End was the residence in the 1740s of the poet and physician Mark Akenside (1721-70).

Greville Estate

The Abbey Farm estate in **Kilburn** was purchased in 1819 by Fulke Greville Howard as a speculation. Two parcels of land at opposite ends of the estate were quickly leased to different developers, that by the Edgware Road to the builder George Pocock. Pocock set out to create an exclusive residential area – the Greville Estate – which straddled the border between Hampstead and St Marylebone; Greville Place, begun as a cul-de-sac into the fields, now forms the borough boundary. Various difficulties were encountered, however, and by 1825 only half a dozen large villas in the Greville Place area had been built.

There was a hiatus until

Golders Hill Mansion, destroyed by a landmine in 1941.

The acquisition of Golders Hill Park, recorded in The Times *22 March, 1900.*

Annie Besant.

Colonel Arthur Upton inherited the estate in 1846. He was able to grant 99-year leases and Greville Road and other streets were then laid out, including Mortimer Crescent named after his land agent. George Orwell (1903-50) lived in a damp flat at No.10 in 1943-44 and the social reformer Annie Besant (1847-1933) was at No.12 between 1876-1883. In 1877 she was tried with Charles Bradlaugh for obscenity for attempting to publish a book on birth control. At its northern end, formerly Alexandra Road, lived the mistress of Edward VII, Lillie Langtry (1853-1929), who had twelve gallons of milk delivered on Thursdays for a weekly bath and who has now given her name to council housing here. The essential church – St Mary's in Priory Road – was begun in 1857; during the 1860s it was briefly one of the leading ritualistic churches in London.

After World War One many houses were subdivided and in the 1930s there were many applications from speculators who wished to demolish large

Lillie Langtry as Rosalind in As You Like It.

houses and redevelop sites for blocks of flats. For example, Mayfield in Mortimer Crescent was replaced in 1934 by Hillsborough Court a block of 112 flats. The **Kilburn Priory** area was redeveloped after the wartime bombing.

The *Ham & High*

The weekly *Hampstead and Highgate Express* was founded at Hampstead in 1860. Known as the 'Ham and High' and vigorously independent, it was edited from 1862 for some 35 years by George Jealous, whose neighbour's schoolboy son Alfred Harmsworth, later Viscount Northcliffe, wrote for the newspaper in 1880. Ownership passed to trustees in the 1930s, then to the Goss family, and in 1964 to Home Counties Newspapers. The paper had two outstanding editors after World War Two – John Parkhurst and his successor, Gerry Isaaman, who in his nearly 40 years with the *Ham & High* was editor for 25 years.

The paper ceased to be

47

George Samuel Jealous, editor of the Ham & High *for 35 years.*

The Ham & High, *then published from the Steam Printing Works at Holly Mount, announces its 1,000th edition.*

Hampstead Cemetery

In the early 1870s it was clear that the parish burial grounds in Church Row would be insufficient to meet the needs of a growing population. The Hampstead burial board, recently set up at the instigation of the medical officer of health, bought twenty acres of pastureland at **Fortune Green** in 1874 at a cost of £7,000 to form Hampstead cemetery. The land was part of the 50-acre Flitcroft estate, once owned by the eponymous architect, and then by his son Henry who died in 1826.

Roughly eleven acres were consecrated in 1876, while the remainder was left for non-Anglicans. A Gothic style chapel for each portion, designed by Charles Bell (who is buried in the cemetery), straddled the division and a mortuary was erected. In 1901 another five acres were added,

independent and in 2000 was bought by Archant, the UK's largest independently-owned regional media business. Recently described as "the tribal noticeboard of the chattering classes", it remains essential reading for all who care about what happens, or may happen, in Hampstead.

For many years the paper was produced at Hampstead's only printing works in the former Baptist chapel in **Holly Mount**. The staff moved in 1961 to new offices in Perrin's Court, and then in 1988 to **Avenue Road** in **Swiss Cottage**.

Hampstead Brewery

Hampstead Brewery was located behind the King of Bohemia pub on Hampstead High Street. It was founded in 1720 by John Vincent. By the 1760s his son owned at least four pubs plus another brewery on the site of the junction of High Street with Heath Street. A popular local brewery, it employed nearly 200 people at the end of the 1920s, but shut in 1931.

The former entrance to the brewery, inscribed 'rebuilt 1869', can still be seen in High Street; it now leads to Old Brewery Mews.

The Hampstead Brewery, located behind the King of Bohemia in the High Street, depicted in 1872.

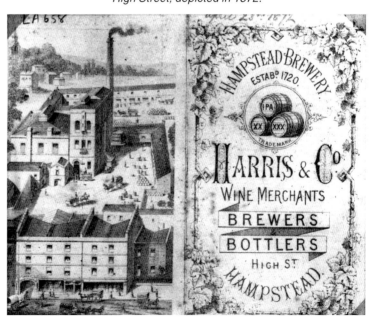

Hampstead Cemetery at Fortune Green. From The Builder *25 November, 1876.*

purchased from the adjoining Burgess Park estate at a rather more expensive £15,000.

There are over 6,000 people buried here. Many artistic people of note were among the early arrivals, including the artists Kate Greenaway and Edwin Long, and the architect Banister Fletcher senior (of Woodchurch Road). Other Hampstead celebrities include George Jealous, proprietor and editor of the **Ham and High**, and two entrepreneurs who lived at the foot of Fitzjohn's Avenue, Frank Debenham and Samuel Palmer. The pioneer of antiseptic surgery, Lord Lister, was buried here in 1912, declining an interment in Westminster Abbey because he preferred to lie here, next to his wife, Agnes. Other pioneers included the children's writer Florence Upton, creator of the golliwog, who had lived in Fellows Road. The queen of the music halls, Marie Lloyd was interred here.

There are some curious monuments, such as an organ-shaped tomb and one inscribed entirely in shorthand, but the most spectacular is the triangular grave commissioned by an Italian chef, Bianchi, for his opera-singer wife who died in childbirth in 1936.

Hampstead Cricket Club

Started as the St John's Wood club in 1867, the HCC changed its name a decade later after a move to what was to become Lymington Road, where a ground was leased from the Lord of the Manor. By 1924 the surrounding area was fully built up and the landlord warned the Club that they must buy or quit. £25,000 was quickly raised in a popular appeal led by the local celebrity, Sir Gerald **du Maurier**. £5,000 came from The Hall School, in exchange for fifteen years' use of the grounds. During the Second World War, the RAF Balloon Section took over part of the grounds and the pavilion. In 1949 the club claimed to have produced more fine players than any other non-county club in England. In the 2008 league season all three of the HCC teams retained their places in the top divisions of the Middlesex County Cricket League.

A hockey section of the HCC, which had played at Lymington Road, became independent in 1894 as Hampstead Hockey Club. This became London's leading hockey side before the First World War, but played outside the borough.

The HCC is now merged with the Cumberland Lawn Tennis Club, which arrived in adjoining Alvanley Gardens in 1903, before the road was built. This club had begun in 1880, when ten men played regularly on a court in Regent's Park and christened their club after nearby Cumberland Terrace. As with the HCC the club first leased the ground from the Lord

Hampstead Cricket Club and their womenfolk. Date unknown.

of the Manor and then bought it from him in the 1920s. The clubhouse built at this time has been progressively enlarged, and similarly the Open Tournament, inaugurated in 1927, has now grown to an important spring event in the annual Wimbledon warm-up.

Hampstead Dinner Club

Hampstead Dinner Club was founded in December 1784 as an association of the town's main residents. The Vestry chiefly comprised tradesmen and real influence in Hampstead probably lay with the wealthy members of this monthly gathering.

The club's first meeting took place at the Long Room, **Well Walk**. Each member was to pay 4s. whether he turned up or not, plus those who did also paid 1s. into a poor box. They later moved into the new **Assembly Rooms**, where they were supplied by the landlord of the adjoining Holly Bush. Members in 1799 included the

Lord Chancellor (Lord Loughborough), the Master of the Rolls (later Lord Alvanley), and Spencer Perceval.

The club lost much of its prestige and its last meeting was held in July 1859 when after an excellent dinner of turtle, venison and champagne, it declared itself dissolved.

Hampstead Football Club

Harlequins Rugby Football Club was originally called Hampstead Football Club. In the 1869/70 season (three years after the club's foundation) they moved from Hampstead Heath and subsequently renamed themselves Harlequins, thus enabling them to keep the HFC monogram. Some of the best known names in English rugby have represented Harlequins.

Another Hampstead rugby football club originated in 1887 as the Crescent club. It changed its name to Hampstead Crescent in 1891 and simply to Hampstead in 1897. Its ground

was at Claremont Road, Cricklewood by 1930.

Today, Hampstead Football Club is the name of a youth soccer club founded in 1998. It fields 32 teams who play in local leagues, with six girls' teams.

Hampstead Green

At the junction of Haverstock Hill and Pond Street, this really was a green, fringed at the south-east by the old George Inn (that had been built by the **Hollow Tree**) and several Georgian houses. One was Bartrams House, whose name derived from the medieval holding called Bartrams recalling a family who held land in the area in the century up to the Black Death of c. 1348. Sir Rowland Hill (1795-1879), best known today as the originator of the Penny Post, lived in the house for thirty years until his death in 1879. Hill is remembered in the name of the adjoining cul-de-sac. His son sold the house to the Metropolitan Asylums Board,

Bartrams House on Hampstead Green, home of Rowland Hill.

who used it for a nurses' home. The building was demolished in 1902 when Hampstead General Hospital was erected on the site.

Next door was Tensleys, reputedly the lodgings in the 1830s of the French diplomat Talleyrand (1754-1838). It was the home in the 1850s of Francis Palgrave (1824-97), compiler of *The Golden Treasury*. He was also Deputy Keeper of Public Records and local historians have him to thank for thwarting official plans to destroy the decennial census returns. Later the house was home to S S Teulon (1812-73), the maverick architect of **St Stephen's church**, which had been built on the centre of the green by 1873. By then the charm of the area had been destroyed by the spread of sheds that made up the Fever Hospital (see **Hospitals**).

Hampstead, Grenada

On the beautiful estate in St David's on the Caribbean island of Grenada, Dr David Pitt (1913-94), the civil rights campaigner and Labour politician was born. In the 1959 general election, he was the first black West Indian UK parliamentary candidate, standing in the Labour interest for Hampstead. He was unsuccessful, but two years later, in 1961, he was elected to the LCC and in 1974 he was the first black person to become chair of the GLC. His home was at No.6 Heath Drive, where he died. In 1975 he was created Baron Pitt of Hampstead in Greater London and of Hampstead in Grenada.

Hampstead Heath

Famous for its wild landscape and expansive views, an inspiration to artists, writers, naturalists and day-trippers alike, the Heath contributes greatly to Hampstead's distinctive character. Less than half of today's open space of some 800 acres called Hampstead Heath lies within Hampstead.

It was first recorded as 'a certain heath' in 1312, and was called Hampstead Heath by Tudor times – in 1543 when its springs were to supply London with water and in 1597 when the herbalist John Gerard described plants which he had found there, encouraging many other plant hunters to visit the Heath.

The sandy ridge that runs from Highgate to Hampstead rests on a belt of sandy clay, underlain by water-resistant London Clay. This led to many springs, and, partly as a result of man-made excavations, swampy hollows. Not suitable for crops, the medieval heath was left mainly as rough moorland, used by commoners for grazing, gathering, and digging for sand and brick clay.

Digging and quarrying continued for centuries. During the 19th century, there was an increasing demand for high quality Bagshot Sand, for use in building and iron foundry casts. Lords of the Manor found the sale of this sand very profitable, not least Sir Thomas Maryon Wilson, who sold a ¼ acre of sand and ballast in strips along Spaniard's Road to the Midland Railway Company in 1866-67. Exploit-ation ceased when the Heath became public property, but in 1939 large pits were dug near the Vale of Health and on Sandy Heath to fill sandbags. The new pits were filled with rubble at the end of the war and their sites were thereafter marked only by different flora.

The Heath was also of value as a commanding height near London. It was the site of a

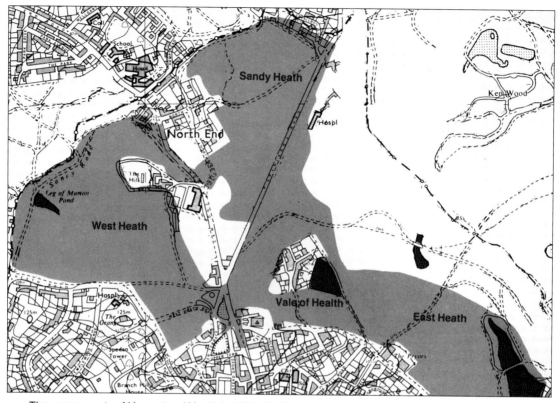

The components of Hampstead Heath in 1871. Parliament Hill and Kenwood, lying to the east and not marked on the map, are historically not part of the Heath, and were acquired later.

beacon, erected as part of an early warning system by 1576, and was later used both for military manoeuvres and firing practice. The height of the Heath, hence its fine outlook and healthy air, was what recommended it to the 18th-century mind, but the Romantic poets and artists, starting with Leigh Hunt, were to praise its scenery. They popularised the Heath and as early as 1829, a writer from Gray's Inn stressed the need for all classes to escape from noise and dirt to one of the few remaining "lungs of the metropolis". Day trippers were to come in their droves later in the century, and the phenomenon known as **'Appy 'Ampstead** arose.

The status of the Heath was for centuries ill-defined. It was nominally part of the Lord of the Manor's property and in the 19th century he employed a Heath Keeper to stop unauthorized people pasturing animals and prevent the theft of turf (a conical Keeper's hut – the Ice House – can be found east of the Vale of Health). The Heath was encroached upon only with the Lord's consent but commoners and copyholders with rights to use the Heath often challenged his actions in granting it away or building upon it. Much of Hampstead town was built on enclosures from the Heath. Shortly after the Wells opened, in 1703 it was noted that 27 acres supporting more than 50 houses had been taken. For the next 150 years and more the Heath was further reduced by the spread of the town, of outlying settlements, notably the **Vale of Health** and **Littleworth**, or of private residences such as the Firs near the **Spaniards**.

The public acquisition of the Heath in 1872 ended more than forty years of uncertainty. Sir Thomas Maryon Wilson, restricted by his father's will to granting leases of no more than 21 years on his Hampstead property, had sought wider powers through successive Estate Bills, all of which were defeated. His proposals alarmed substantial local residents, who success-fully presented them to a wider public as threats to an increasingly popular Heath. The battles in the press and Parliament left Sir Thomas with a long lasting reputation as a would-be despoiler.

*Sir Thomas Maryon Wilson,
the 7th baronet.*

Sir Thomas's first Estate Bill was withdrawn from the House of Commons in 1829, after local opposition and a campaign in the press on the need to preserve open space. In reality, his desire to obtain the power to grant 99-year building leases on all his Hampstead lands did not arise from plans for the Heath as it then existed, where the copyholders could insist on their rights of pasturage, but for his 60 acres of exclusive freehold which were later known as East Park. Building there, along the St Pancras boundary, would have hemmed in the Heath and threatened the views of many Hampstead gentry and of Lord Mansfield from Kenwood. Lord Mansfield therefore joined the opposition and in 1830 helped to defeat a second, modified, Bill in the House of Lords. It was probably the House's first division on an Estate Bill. Despite Sir Thomas's insistence that he had no plans for the Heath itself, all his succeeding attempts over the next three decades to obtain an Estate Act were thwarted.

Public purchase was urged on both the Metropolitan Board of Works (MBW) and the government in 1856 by the reformed Hampstead vestry, unsuccessfully, but the MBW was given new powers by the Metropolitan Commons Act, 1866. This was after pressure from the Commons Pre-servation Society, which included Gurney **Hoare**, Philip Le Breton, and other Hampstead campaigners among its members. In Hampstead the danger was now acute because the exasperated Sir Thomas had started to commercialize the Heath, by building on the summit and selling the sand along Spaniard's Road. East Park was also despoiled, by brickfields. A law suit was taken out in Chancery in 1866 by Gurney Hoare and two other copyholders against Sir Thomas, which was ended only by the latter's death in 1869. His brother and heir was able to break the restrictive settlement, and in 1872 the MBW felt compelled to buy the Heath, authorized by the Hampstead Heath Act of 1871.

Expansion of the area in public ownership was largely in response to the spread of housing across open countryside to the north and west of the Heath. The Heath was doubled in size when East Park, Parliament Hill and Fields, and part of Lord Mansfield's estate was acquired in 1889. **Golders Hill Park** at North End was added in 1898. It adjoined West Heath but mostly lay in Hendon, as did the 80 acres known as Hampstead Heath Extension bought in 1907. This was part of **Wyldes** farm, the rest of which was taken for Hampstead Garden Suburb. The last major addition in the 1920s was the Kenwood estate in Highgate.

By 1875, with the scars of excavation largely grown over, the MBW won praise for a judicious neglect which had not made the Heath "prim or park-like", but there have been campaigns ever since to ensure its wildness. To this end in 1897 local residents formed what is now the **Heath and Hampstead Society**. And vigilance was also needed to protect against tall or incongruous buildings overlooking the Heath. The redevelopment on the bombed site north of Jack Straw's Castle was averted by its purchase for a car park.

After the abolition of the LCC's successor, the GLC, Hampstead Heath passed in 1989 to the City of London, who manage it today, dedicated to the Heath's natural appear-ance, while maintaining accessibility and the health of its environment.

Since it became public property, the Heath has been extremely popular. The City of London estimates that at present between 8 and 10 million people come here every year. The range of wildlife is impressive for an urban site visited by so many people. Kingfishers, reed warblers and all three species of British woodpecker breed. Even alien green parakeets have settled on the Heath. Over 300 species of fungi have been recorded and it is one of the best places in London to see a number of species of bats.

Many come here to enjoy sporting activities. The **Hampstead ponds** were used for skating in the Victorian period and continue in use for open-air bathing and swim-ming. In winter tobogganers

The Hampstead Heath Station disaster, depicted in the Penny Illustrated Paper in 1892.

have taken to the snowy slopes. Cricket took place on West Heath, while there are still football pitches and tennis courts. And Hampstead Heath now enjoys a rather unfortunate reputation for more carnal pleasures.

Hampstead Heath Station

Opened as part of the Hampstead Junction Railway (later North London line) in 1860, the station quickly attracted large crowds drawn by the appeal of **'Appy 'Ampstead**. It was ill-suited to cope with such numbers and a terrible accident occurred at Easter 1892 as people dashed into the building to escape a sudden heavy shower. Barratt wrote that "immense numbers pressed forward to the staircase leading to the up platform and, being unable to force a passage because of a ticket collector's box at the bottom, were thrown into such confusion that it was impossible for all to extricate themselves". Eight people were crushed to death and many injured. The station was remodelled as a result, with an upstairs ticket office.

In 1968 the original single-storey brick building was replaced by a drab modern affair. The rail bridge was widened at the same time which prompted local protest that suspected a plan to make the road a Hampstead by-pass, taking in some of the Heath. This gave birth to the **South End Green** Association, which has thrived ever since. A plaque on the bridge notes that it replaced a 20-ft wide cast-iron bridge built in 1864.

The present station is now part of London Overground: this was launched here by the

Hampstead Heath station at the beginning of the 20th century. The pepperpot building in the centre of the picture, which looks west, was the engine house of the Hampstead Water Company. This pumped water to Kentish Town and Camden Town, and was demolished in 1907.

Mayor of London in November 2007.

Hampstead Magistrates Court

The Court was built in 1913 at the corner of Downshire Hill and Rosslyn Hill. Until the late 1980s the Hampstead Court was unique in London in being an entirely lay court, with no stipendiaries. This was a legacy of the system of justice that had prevailed in the town since the 18th century. A large number of rich men lived in Hampstead, and families like the **Hoares** were keen to preserve its 'gentlemanly rurality'. It had been customary for Hampstead JPs to hold court in their own house, often on their own and with no legal assistance. The lock-up below **Cannon Hall** reflects this practice.

During the 19th century as Hampstead grew into a provincial town, the powers of JPs were extended and more detailed record keeping was necessary. Courts were held at the **Workhouse** and then in a room above the police station in Rosslyn Hill, until the

purpose-built Court opened nearby. The nature of the Hampstead magistracy was changing from its traditional role as a community peacekeeper to a more strictly judicial one hearing a far wider range of cases. The separate Hampstead Court finally closed in 1998.

Hampstead Manor

In a charter of c.974 King Edgar granted five hides of land (approx. 600 acres) in Hampstead to his faithful servant Mangoda for life. The same five hides were given by King Ethelred the Unready to Westminster Abbey in 986. The charter recording this is not genuine but it is a record made at Westminster during the King's lifetime. The charters of confirmation, by Ethelred in 998 and by Edward the Confessor in 1065 and 1066, are generally agreed to be spurious, the last two probably the work of Prior Osbert de Clare in the 12th century. Nevertheless a genuine grant almost certainly lay behind the fabrications and by the time of Domesday Book Westminster Abbey held the manor of Hampstead as five hides.

In 1086, then, Hampstead was valued at only 50 shillings, a small farm with fodder for 100 pigs in a clearing of the vast Middlesex Forest. The farm nevertheless furnished the monks of Westminster with fresh produce throughout the Middle Ages. From 1259 until it was surrendered in 1540 the abbey administered the manor directly, via a bailiff or steward, as the Lords of the Manor, the Abbots, were absentees. The secular Lords that followed the dissolution of the monasteries were also absentees.

The Wroth family owned the manor until it was sold in 1620 to Sir Baptist Hicks, mercer and moneylender and later Lord Campden (note the 'p'). His family in 1643 founded a charity for the poor of Hampstead. So did the Earl of Gainsborough's family, who inherited the manor; they donated some land around **Well Walk** in 1698. Their gifts are now united in the **Wells and Campden Trust**. During the 18th century the manor passed to the Maryon Wilson family. The land was generally leased, but the lords reserved to themselves the manor court. There was never a manor house, but a manor farm existed in Frognal.

Small pieces on the edge of the demesne were sold off, mostly in the early 19th century. Further sales were prevented until 1869 under the terms of the will of the first Sir Thomas Maryon Wilson and even when the death of the second Sir Thomas in 1869 released the land, little was sold. Most of the estate was developed on building leases. The largest portion sold was East Heath Park, which in 1889

was added to the Heath, already acquired by the Metropolitan Board of Works. Although the manor as such is now defunct, The Maryon Wilsons still own a slice of Hampstead.

In the 17th century the manor pound was in the High Street, probably on its west side at the upper end of **Slyes**, and later moved to **Littleworth**. In 1787 a new pound was built in a hollow opposite Whitestone pond. The jaw bones of a whale formed the supports of the gate until the early 20th century. The manor stocks, used as late as 1831, stood at the bottom of Flask Walk next to the watchhouse there.

Hampstead Museum

Founded by local historians Christopher and Diana Wade in 1979 to coincide with the reopening of **Burgh House**, in which it is housed. Community groups including Camden Libraries, Hampstead Artists Council and the **Heath and Hampstead Society** donated materials and the collection continues to grow.

In 2002 Hampstead Museum was awarded a Heritage Lottery Grant which allowed for a refurbishment of the permanent exhibition and stores. Today the museum is staffed by a part-time curator, and puts on a range of lectures, walks, and changing exhibitions.

Hampstead Parochial School

Hampstead's parish school had unusual origins, founded by a local society of gentlemen called the **Philo-Investigists** who in 1787 established a Sunday school when the movement was being popularised by Robert Raikes. They chose twelve boys and twelve girls from the Sunday school to attend two day schools for the poor which they set up in 1790. The first master was Thomas Mitchell, whose gravestone in the parish churchyard bears the society's triangular symbol.

The day boys were taught the 3 Rs, while the day girls were taught reading, knitting, and sewing. From 1815 the school was governed by the Parochial School Society, which decided on education in accordance with doctrines of the Church of England, although admission was without a religious test. The girls moved to a new building at the corner of Holly Walk and Mount Vernon, while the boys from 1826 had a schoolroom in the **workhouse** garden. In 1856 new schools were built in Holly Bush Vale. After World War Two, these reopened in 1951 as a voluntary aided primary school, which retains close links with the parish church.

Hampstead Ponds

In 1543/44 the City Corporation obtained an Act of Parliament to make use of "dyvers great and plentifull sprynges at Hampstede Hethe" and other places within five miles of the City. Nothing was done until 1589-90 when Sir John Hart was Lord Mayor. He accompanied the herbalist John Gerard

The Hampstead Ponds c. 1905, with the houses of South Hill Park in the background.
To the left is the slope of Parliament Hill.

to view the springs and 'attempted' some unspecified works, which must have been to impound the water from the springs by building an embankment in the valley below the summit of the Heath and establishing the reservoirs known as Hampstead Ponds. The scheme was intended to supply the City and scour the River Fleet but failed.

A century later William Paterson (1658-1719), founder of the Bank of England, and others leased the ponds on 10 January 1693 on a renewable 21-year lease in an enterprise called the Hampstead Water Company, a non-statutory body. A string of ponds were excavated in Highgate. In 1777 another reservoir pond was added and water also taken from a pond at the **Vale of Health**. However, the Hampstead Water Company was never one of the main suppliers of water in London and as population increased its supply proved insufficient.

Hampstead itself was not supplied by the company, whose customers were primarily in Kentish Town and south towards Tottenham Court Road. In the mid 1830s it sank a 320 ft well into chalk between Hampstead Ponds Nos. 1 and 2, with a steam pumping engine housed in an octagonal pepperpot tower *(see p. 55)*. After the company was taken over by the New River Company (who used the water for non-domestic purposes only) the engine was removed in 1858, and No.1 pond was filled in in the early 1890s having become a public nuisance. The tower was adapted as a residence but demolished in 1907.

Other ponds on the Heath, not connected with the Water Company, include Leg of **Mutton Pond** and **Whitestone Pond** and Viaduct Pond, crossed by a viaduct dating from the mid 1840s and created from a swampy valley as part of Sir Thomas Maryon Wilson's

abortive preparations to build on his freehold land at East Heath. Skaters traditionally used ponds on the Heath and a club skated on Viaduct Pond in the 1870s and 1880s.

Swimming has long been popular in the ponds. In 1814 J J Park noted they "have been fatal to many incautious bathers, owing to the sudden shelving of their sides". The Heath now boasts three unique and internationally famous bathing ponds: the Ladies', Men's and Mixed Ponds, only available to competent swimmers. The first two are in Highgate; the Mixed Pond, otherwise Hampstead No.3 Pond, is open to the public in summer. In winter, because no lifeguards are present, only members of the Hampstead Heath Winter Swimming Club are allowed to swim there.

Hampstead Ponds were famous in literature because Dickens has Samuel Pickwick read a paper entitled 'Speculations on the Source of the Hampstead Ponds, with some observations on the Theory of Tittlebats'.

Hampstead Scientific Society

The Hampstead Astronomical and Scientific Society was founded in 1899, having been given a telescope which it placed on a site on East Heath granted by the LCC. The society, which met at **Stanfield House**, was divided into astronomical, photographic, and natural history sections. In 1909 it constructed an observatory and meteorological station on top of the covered reservoir near the summit of the Heath. Sited near Whitestone Pond, one of the highest points in London, this was thought a good spot for stargazing, which continues here to this day. The public are admitted during winter evenings and visitors can enjoy the use of an original six-inch Thomas Cook of York refracting telescope, which dates back to the turn of the 20th century, one of the earliest high-tech instruments of its kind. The weather station has been checked daily since 1910, providing the longest continuous record of meteorological readings in the country.

Hampstead Square

Turned into a polygon by the building of **Christ Church** this was once a rectangular grove, shown on the 1762 map, where strolling players performed. It contains several beautiful, self-assured 18th-century houses and merges into Elm Row. There a grand terrace, built in 1720, contains No.3, the home in 1879-80 of Sir Henry Cole (1808-82), who helped found

Hampstead Square c. 1901, drawing by A R Quinton.

the V&A and is said to have begun the practice of sending Christmas cards. He did not enjoy his time in Hampstead and did not stay long.

Hampstead Theatre

The Hampstead Theatre Club was begun in 1959 at a hall behind the **Everyman**. The hall, given by the vicar, was also used by scouts and mother-and-toddler groups and the vicar eventually asked the theatre to leave. The Artistic Director, James Roose-Evans, persuaded Hampstead Council to provide a prefabricated civic theatre, seating 160, at Swiss

Cottage, whither the club moved in 1962.

Although the building was meant to be temporary and conditions were cramped it was the theatre's home for forty years. During this time, under successive directors, Hampstead Theatre developed a national and international reputation for the presentation of new plays, many of which have transferred to the West End. A new building – with much improved facilities – was opened in 2003. Built by Bennetts Association it includes the Michael Frayn Space, a dedicated arena for the theatre's Creative Learning

Hampstead Theatre in 2009.

programme, which has enabled the theatre to expand massively its work for young people.

Hampstead Tube

The Charing Cross, Euston, & Hampstead Railway had been authorized to build a tube railway from Charing Cross to Heath Street in 1893 but nothing was done until its powers passed to the American tycoon, Charles Tyson Yerkes (1837-1905), who formed the Underground Group. Since it would offer a fast link to the West End, his proposed line to Hampstead was welcomed by many, unlike his plans to burrow under the Heath. One letter to *The Times* even suggested that moisture would drain from the trees and grass of the Heath.

A projected station to serve the summit of the Heath, near Jack Straw's Castle, was opposed both by the local authority and the local preservationists. Its site was moved to a point just across the boundary, where platforms but not access shafts were built for a station whose intended name was changed from North End to Bull and Bush. The station never opened. In the event, the new line, called the Hampstead Tube, terminated beyond the Heath at a rural crossroads at Golders Green.

There were stations in the parish called Chalk Farm, at the foot of Haverstock Hill; **Belsize Park**, and Hampstead, at the corner of High Street and Heath Street. All were designed by Leslie Green in the ox-blood glazed bricks used for all surface stations in the group.

Hampstead station was opened on its present site on 22 June 1907 by David Lloyd George. It replaced half a dozen houses and shops and, symbolically perhaps, a watering trough for horses. Travel was free for the first day, attracting some 127,500 passengers in the seven hours it operated. Barratt recorded in 1912 that the electric tube railway brought over three million passengers to Hampstead annually. The platforms at Hampstead are the deepest in London (192 ft below street level), which made it a popular wartime air raid shelter.

After the Hampstead Tube had been linked with the City & South London Railway

A bird's-eye view of the proposed Hampstead Tube, which terminated at Golders Green and Highgate. The South Kentish Town station building remains, though the station closed in 1924. The line became officially part of the Northern line in 1938.

A promotional postcard featuring some artistic highlights of Hampstead.

Company under an Act of 1913, the line was known as the Edgware, Highgate & Morden line. From 1938 it formed part of the Northern line.

Hampstead Village

Tourist Hampstead is now usually called Hampstead Village but was for centuries known as Hampstead Town. It has not only kept its pre-Victorian street pattern, very intricate and full of passages and steps, but many of its early houses as well, so that it is a joy to wander here. Here are some of London's finest, unspoilt examples of domestic Georgian architecture.

By the 15th century many of the customary tenements had passed to London merchants and gentry, some of whom began to occupy or lease them. From Tudor times houses were rebuilt in brick e.g. **Chicken House** on what is now Rosslyn Hill.

Development northward and eastward was on the Heath, technically waste but land taken from the waste became copyhold. Cottages and sheds were put up in a haphazard way and the passages to such enclosures and the spaces between them became roads and squares. With the steep and uneven nature of the ground this gave rise to the odd street pattern.

Hampstead's pure air was acknowledged in the 16th century and its mineral waters were known about from the mid 17th century, but the settlement only rapidly developed into a town once the **Wells** were exploited commercially. **Well Walk** pushed development farther eastward, and inns, shops, and lodging houses sprang up throughout Hampstead town to cater for the influx of visitors. The area to the west, on ancient copyhold and freehold land, was also developed in the early 18th century, notably by Richard Hughes of Holborn who began **Church Row**.

Hampstead's attractions as a permanent residence increased. By 1810 there were more than 500 dwellings in Hampstead town, many of them fine new houses, for example those built on the broad piece of waste south of Pond Street, later called **Hampstead Green**. In 1811 the Vestry bought 2½ acres to extend the parish churchyard; it sold off the northern portion of the land where Prospect, Benham's and Holly Places were built.

The then Lord of the Manor, Sir Thomas Maryon Wilson (d.1821) encouraged building on copyhold land, the largest development on which was the **Downshire Hill triangle**. His

son was prevented from exploiting his estate in the same way, and until his death in 1869 building did not keep pace with demand and the alleys and courts in central Hampstead became over-crowded, and deteriorated into **slums**, swept away under the Town Improvements in the 1880s.

By then, Hampstead had seen another burst of building activity. On the Maryon Wilson demesne lands to the south and west, enfranchised copyhold land became covered in a great swathe of red-brick Queen Anne style houses, aimed squarely at the prosperous professional class. The frontages of shops in Heath and High streets were rebuilt and Hampstead charities were active in erecting dwellings for the lower classes, who were also supplied with baths and wash-houses.

By the turn of the 20th century the old established gentry had left Hampstead town and in the next few years nearly all the available land had been built over, leaving room only for infilling or rebuilding. Most wealthy people lived in the newer districts or overlooking the Heath, leaving much of Hampstead town to flats. In the 1930s it had an air of faded gentility, captured by contemporary writers such as Vita Sackville-West. But it was in this decade that its avant-garde and politically left-wing intellectual tradition became firmly established.

Gentrification became much more prevalent after **World War Two**, during which central Hampstead was largely spared bombing, apart from **New End**. From the mid 1960s the working class retreated from central Hampstead and by 1975 ordinary small shops were being replaced by chain stores, in what by then was called Hampstead village, a conservation area.

Hampstead Volunteers

Volunteer fighting units emerged during the threat of Napoleonic invasion. Gentry kitted themselves out with uniforms and rifles and marched in the streets with as many of the local tradesmen and lower social orders as could be mustered to follow them. In 1798 the engraver and publisher Josiah Boydell (1752-1817), nephew of Alderman Boydell and living in West End, founded the Loyal Hampstead Association, who drilled and fired their muskets on the Heath. It was disbanded after the peace of 1802, but the following year the Hampstead Volunteers Corps was formed, with 700 members commanded by Boydell, who resigned in 1806. The Volunteers were disbanded in 1813. Their target ground on East Heath was used by companies from outside the parish, to the anger of residents.

A new volunteer force was recruited in 1859, upon a renewed threat of French invasion. It trained in the paddock of **The Hill** and in the winter in the **Assembly Rooms**. It joined corps from Highgate and Hornsey and in 1862 was entitled the 3rd Middlesex (Hampstead) Rifle Volunteers, taking a lease of the former pump room and chapel in **Well Walk** as a drill hall. It ended its separate existence in 1880, on becoming the Hampstead detachments of the 3rd Middlesex Rifle Volunteers. After the surrender in 1881 of the drill hall for demolition the Hampstead detachments had smaller, unsuitable premises in High Street. In 1888 a hall was built in Holly Bush Vale, becoming the **Everyman** Theatre after World War One. Men from the Rifle Volunteers fought in the Boer War and helped form the Hampstead Athletic Club in 1880 which was active into the Edwardian period.

The East Middlesex Militia had Hampstead as its headquarters from 1858, taking over **Burgh House** for its officers' mess. Barracks blocks were built either side of the front garden, used as the parade ground. Married quarters were added in Willow Road in 1863; these later became Willow Hall. In 1881 locals resisted plans to upgrade Hampstead as the brigade headquarters and the Militia departed.

Sir Henry Harben

The first Mayor of Hampstead, Harben (1823-1911) was born in Bloomsbury in 1823. He joined the Prudential and persuaded the directors to offer assurance for the working classes, then considered a

Volunteers out in force on the Heath in the late 1850s.

Sir Henry Harben, Hampstead's first mayor.

pointless undertaking. Although initially the Prudential found the expense of house-to-house collection almost ruinous, it was by 1891 insuring one person in four in the United Kingdom. As a major shareholder in the Prudential, Harben became wealthy, and contributed to numerous causes.

He lived in Hampstead from 1865, and from 1870 at Seaford Lodge, No.2 Fellows Road, a large stuccoed four-square house replete with Corinthian pilasters. Harben served as a member of the Hampstead Vestry from 1874, represented the area on the Metropolitan Board of Works from 1880 to 1889, and on the London County Council until 1894. He funded the building among others of the central public library in Arkwright Road (now the **Camden Arts Centre**) and a wing of the Hampstead General Hospital. On the MBW he was instrumental in getting the board to agree the purchase of East Park, and he participated in the campaigns to add the **Golders Hill** estate to Hampstead Heath. His

daughter Mrs Mary Wharrie inherited some of his fortune and his generosity. Her name lives on in the Wharrie Cabman's Shelter at **Hampstead Green**, which she funded in 1935, with the residue to be used for other charitable purposes.

Haverstock Hill

Haverstock Hill is thought to be the 'Foxhangra' mentioned in the 10th-century records of Hampstead, a hanger being a wood on a steepish hill, but its first appearance on a map is in John Norden's *Middlesex* of 1593. It then and for some time afterwards referred to the area surrounding the roadway, which was itself often called Hampstead Hill or the London Road.

The name Haverstock might derive from the Latin *averia*, meaning a pasture, but it more likely comes from the Anglo-Saxon words *haver*, meaning oats (cf. Haverhill) and stock, a place. Oats formed part of the Belsize estate's rent to Westminster Abbey in the 18th century and were indeed grown in this place.

It was some time before the

roadway above Chalk Farm became known as Haverstock Hill and only in 1876 was it officially designated as such by the Post Office throughout its present length. The present numbering also dates from that year.

In the 18th century a small settlement near the **Load of Hay** that included **Steele's Cottage** stood alone among fields but it was engulfed in the next by the spread of housing up the hill from the Chalk Farm toll gate (removed in 1864). This consisted mostly of solid 19th-century villas, but many of these have given way to modern blocks. Nevertheless, several interesting older buildings remain.

Above England's Lane there is a small but busy shopping parade and a series of cafés and restaurants spread out onto the wider pavements, which lends this stretch of Haverstock Hill a continental air.

Nearby is the old **Town Hall** but dominating the landscape here is the Premier Travel Lodge, formerly the Post House Hotel, which opened in 1970. At the corner of Belsize Grove, stood Bedford Lodge, home of John Maple (1845-1903), owner

The lower reaches of Haverstock Hill c.1905, showing Oxendon church – a building now used by Hampstead Seventh Day Adventists. Maitland Park Road is to the right.

of the furniture store. In an adjoining house, then called No.5 Devonshire Place, lived the railway engineer Robert Stephenson from 1836 to 1842.

By Ornan Road was Ivy Bank, rebuilt as a flamboyant Victorian villa around 1875. While he was developing the road, the tycoon Alfred Ridley Bax used it in 1893 as his headquarters. His sons, (Sir) Arnold and Clifford, distinguished themselves in music and drama respectively.

At the top of Haverstock Hill, by the old **Hampstead Green** is the George pub, first mentioned in the licensing records of 1715. It was noted for its tea gardens and also served as a post office. An even earlier name for the pub was the Great Tree, being next to the famous **Hollow Elm**.

Heath and Hampstead Society

By its own admission the Society comprises fully paid up members of the awkward squad, who keep planning authorities on their toes. It had its origins in the Hampstead Heath Protection Fund Committee set up by 1866 to raise money to try to buy Heath land and continue the legal battle with Sir Thomas Maryon Wilson. His death in 1869 ended the campaign and victory was sealed by an Act of Parliament in 1871 which protected 200 acres of the Heath as an open space for the people of London, under the guardianship of the Metropolitan Board of Works, who bought the Heath the following year.

The MBW was replaced by the LCC who began to 'parkify' the Heath in the 1890s, and the

George Shaw Lefevre (later Lord Eversley), who played a leading part in saving Hampstead Heath and was president of the Hampstead Heath Protection Society 1908-11 and 1921-27.

campaigners who had fought to save it for its wild and natural beauty returned to the fray. In 1896 a petition was begun, signed by a host of distinguished people, including Octavia Hill and Norman Shaw, and supported by the national press. At a public meeting in April 1897 the Committee was resurrected as the Hampstead Heath Protection Society, the first Civic Society in London. Its name has changed over the years.

The Society has been prominent in the various campaigns to add land to the Heath whenever the opportunity has arisen. It has also campaigned to save the fringes of the Heath from development, attempting to preserve the feeling of openness and the beautiful views by objecting to any high-rise building nearby (the Royal Free was the only one that got away). It monitors the wildlife and biodiversity of the Heath

and runs a programme of regular monthly Heath Walks.

As its present name makes clear, however, the Society is also concerned with Hampstead and seeks to protect its unique townscape. It fought various plans up to the 1970s to construct new roads across the area, and has initiated many schemes to improve the local streetscape, refurbishing old street lamps and wrought-iron benches, cleaning and restoring street fountains and wells, and planting new trees. It has worked hard to support local independent shops and businesses.

At the top of Heath Street a slate plaque was erected to mark the Society's centenary in 1997.

Heath House

This fine early-18th-century house faces Whitestone Pond, its setting marred only by an unfortunately placed war memorial on ground donated by the owners. From 1799 it was the home of the Quaker banker **Samuel Hoare** and remained owned by the Hoares until 1876. The house was given its present name when taken in 1888 by the newspaper proprietor Sir Algernon Borthwick, later Baron Glenesk. From 1911 it was inhabited by Viscount (later the Earl of) Iveagh until he moved into and saved Kenwood for the nation. It is still privately owned. Planning permission was granted in 2008 for a luxury neo-classical house in the grounds, designed by Robert Adam, an architect much favoured by Prince Charles.

Heath House by A R Quinton, 1910. The house faces Whitestone Pond.

Robertson, novelist and critic. She was famous for her comment that "Hampstead is not so much a place as a state of mind". The actors Peter O'Toole and his wife Sian Phillips lived at No.98 for many years. The terrace ends beside the neo-Gothic Baptist Church, designed by C G Searle, which opened in 1861. Underneath the chapel were originally school premises specially designed for the Heath Street British Day School; pupils were transferred to New End School in 1907. At the junction with Back Lane is the **Kingswell** development.

Heath Street

One of the two principal streets of the 'village' leading from **Fitzjohn's Avenue** and the top of High Street up to Whitestone Pond and the Heath.

Winding, gently hilly, and lined with handsome houses, off either side is a labyrinth of tiny streets, alleyways and courts. The street name does not appear in the Rate Books until 1831: the northern end was previously called Heath Mount and the rest was included in the High Street. On the 1680 map it formed a broad green, over 100ft wide, extending from the Heath.

Heath Mount was the name of a school at the top of Heath Street, demolished in 1934. Opposite, is the wide pavement outside the old Queen Mary's Maternity Home at No.124, now an annexe of the Royal Free Hospital and the site of the **Upper Flask Tavern**. Here open air art exhibitions were held on summer weekends until 1983.

Lower down is an 18th-century terrace beginning with Guyon House, the home for many years of E Arnot

Heath Street looking north in the 1930s, watercolour by Mary Hill.

The southern end of the street was formed only in the late 1880s to meet the recently constructed Fitzjohn's Avenue. Several courts lead off it. Yorkshire Grey Place, for example, was named in 1994 (with the help of the **Camden History Society**) after an old inn demolished here in the 1880s. Perrin's Walk commemorates the Perrin family who owned property in this area in the early 18th century. Until 1936, this was called Church Walk. The comedian Peter Cook moved here from Church Row in the early 1970s and stayed until his death in 1995. The picturesque No.20 was used by Henry Holiday (1839-1927) as his glassworks: the kiln chimney survives. All the leading Pre-Raphaelites came here to discuss art and his wife Catherine was one of William Morris's chief embroiderers. The Holidays lived at Oak Tree House in Redington Gardens designed by Basil Champneys in 1874. The writer Eleanor Farjeon (1881-1965) later lived at No.20 from 1920 until her death in 1965, remembered for her children's books.

In Perrin's Court lived two famous Hampstead characters. No.1 was home to Bert Matthews, for forty years rat-catcher to Hampstead Borough Council and Pearly King of Hampstead, while in No.3 lived the last local chimney sweep Henry Kippin, born here in 1882. His handcart is preserved in the garden of Burgh House.

High Hill Bookshop

This was a Hampstead institution, strung out over several properties in the High Street. Run by Ian and Mavis Norrie, it was in its time the most comprehensive bookshop in north London and a cultural and intellectual centre. It attracted the custom and friendship of numerous literati and acted as the box office and script office for the infant **Hampstead Theatre**. The late Ian Norrie was never afraid to speak his mind. One sign on the shop's door read "Children of Progressive Parents admitted only on Leads".

High Hill Bookshop closed in 1988.

High Street

The main road up the hill, it was referred to as a high street (*alte strate*) in 1633. It had previously been called Kingswell Street and later enjoyed various names – such as Hampstead Street and Hampstead Hill – which at times also included some or all of the upper part of Heath Street.

Many of the modern shop fronts conceal ancient buildings, such as Old Bank House at No.14, once part of the Three Tuns Tavern. During the period of the Wells there were numerous hostelries catering for the many visitors attracted to Hampstead town, but after the Wells closed most of these closed too. Today there are a mere handful of pubs and bars left in the High Street. The old King's Head pub was renamed the King William IV after the monarch drove through Hampstead in 1835 on his way to a strawberry feast at Ken Wood.

By the 1880s, as the western side concealed decaying property which the Vestry wished to clear away, it was decided to remove all the buildings on that side above

No.72: these had their frontages at just about the middle of the present roadway. Several unsavoury courts and alleys disappeared at the same time.

In recent years the trend has been away from independent businesses to more tourist-oriented concerns and the individual character of the High Street has suffered. McDonalds arrived at No.46 in 1993, despite strong local opposition and after a 13-year campaign for a prime site in Hampstead. Soaring property rents have also helped rob central Hampstead of most of its useful shops, although it features some of the amenities of a High Street. In 1974 local citizens formed the Hampstead Community Trust because of concerns about the loss of independent shops and five years later a community centre was leased at No.78, still flourishing.

Hampstead High Street was home to a number of different automobile dealers and garages over the 20th century. The last of these was the Blue Star Garage south of **Flask Walk**, demolished in the late 1970s. Controversy raged for years around its redeve-lopment but the resultant houses, flats and shops are unassuming.

On the west side is a complex of flats called Green-hill, on the site of a long-lived mansion called The Rookery, which was the home until 1842, of the Longman publishing family. Dame Edith Sitwell lived for three years at Flat 42, Greenhill, moving in 1964 to Keats Grove, where she died.

Nos.6-7 High Street are on the site of Miss Noble's school, where Constable sent his daughters in the 1830s. By Nos.1A-C Maggie Richardson

Hampstead High Street in the 1930s, looking south. Watercolour by Mary Hill.

(1901-1974) sold flowers for sixty years and is commemorated on the wall with a floral plaque.

Maggie Richardson c. 1948, selling flowers in the High Street.

Highwaymen

From the late 17th century to the early 19th century the roads to Hampstead were infested with highwaymen, at least in the popular imagination, fuelled by numerous newspaper reports of assaults. Some places of entertainment provided guards for patrons. The Heath, in particular, was considered dangerous and long remembered for having been chosen for the exemplary display of the body of Francis Jackson, who was hanged in 1674. The gibbet probably stood at the top of the hill leading down to North End, although the 'gibbet elms' depicted in the 19th century were farther down the slope towards the town.

Another highwayman active in the area in Stuart times was Claude Duval who achieved notoriety because when he halted coaches he would, allegedly, dance with lady passengers while the gentlemen hand over their valuables. Platt's Lane was once called Duval's Lane, corrupted to Devil's Lane.

The most famous highwayman, Dick Turpin, is associated with the **Spaniard's**. Here he is said to have stabled Black Bess and to have had a key to a passage to effect his escape. There is absolutely no evidence to support the legend.

Dark roads bred the fear of crime. The *London Chronicle* reported in 1758 that inhabitants had opened a subscription for setting up lamps from Hampstead to Gray's Inn Lane to prevent robberies. The Vestry later recognised that gas lighting was "the most efficient aid in the repression and detection of offenders in the streets and

The Stuart Room at The Hill, then the home of Lord Leverhulme. The drawing is by T Raffles Davison.

highways", but this was in 1823 when the days of the highwayman were all but over.

The Hill

Erected at **Littleworth**, this house in North End Way was advertised in 1779 as lately built and was given by Samuel Hoare to his son Samuel in 1807, when the latter married Elizabeth Fry's sister. The black plaque records that John Gurney Hoare, was born here in 1810 and took a leading part in the battle to save the Heath from development. Tennyson and Wordsworth met for the first time at The Hill in 1845.

The **Hoares** sold the house in 1896 to George Fisher, who rebuilt it and sold it in 1904 to the soap magnate, William Lever (1851-1925), later Lord Leverhulme, who devised the Port Sunlight 'model village' on

the Wirral. He added two wings (one for his art gallery), acquired two neighbouring properties, Cedar Lawn and Heath Lodge, laid out new grounds designed by Thomas Mawson, and built the pergola walk. In 1926, a year after he died, the property passed to the shipping magnate Lord Inverforth (1865-1955) who, thirty years later, bequeathed it to Manor House Hospital. As Inverforth House it became the women's section of the hospital, with around 100 beds, and a home for nursing staff. In 1996-98 the building was converted to luxury apartments, with some new houses to the north.

Since 1963, when it was acquired by the LCC, The Hill Garden has been open to the public, as is the delightful Pergola Walk, now Listed II*. Begun in 1905, the Pergola,

designed to be the setting for Lever's summer parties, required a massive raising of the ground. Fortuitously, the **Hampstead Tube** was being built at the same time and thousands of wagon-loads of spoil were brought here by the contractors, paying the astute Lever a nominal sum for accommodating the material that he needed to realise his dream. After long neglect, it was repaired by the City of London, who added another garden at the foot of the Pergola in 1995.

Hoare Family

A rich Quaker family, prominent in Hampstead society. The family fortune was founded by the banker Samuel Hoare (1751-1825), who lived at **Heath House**. A leading member of the anti-slave trade

67

John Gurney Hoare by George Richmond, 1855.

movement, he helped move the **workhouse** from damp Frognal to healthier New End. Samuel often entertained a literary circle that included Byron, Wordsworth, Joanna Baillie and Scott.

His son, also Samuel, was recognised as the squire of Hampstead and rode down from **The Hill** to the City each day accompanied by his groom. He married Louisa Gurney, the sister of the prison reformer Elizabeth Fry and was also a strong supporter of Clarkson and Wilberforce in their scheme to abolish slavery. He started the fight with the Lord of the Manor over development on the Heath. It was carried on after his death in 1847 by his son John Gurney Hoare, who began the lawsuit with two other copyholders which was important in the successful campaign to 'save' the Heath. Gurney's brother Joseph lived at Child's Hill House and together they took the lead setting up **Christ Church**, and his daughter Margaret managed the North End School in Sandy Road that he founded.

Holford Family

The members of this worthy family were leaders of Hampstead society. Josiah Holford (1727-1817) was patron of the Society of **Philo-Investigists**. His son Charles (1774-1838) bought **Romney's House** for use as **Assembly Rooms**, where he encouraged his friend Constable to give his lectures on the *Origin of Landscape Painting*. He was chairman of the Hampstead Subscription Library and also of the **Hampstead Dinner Club**. He moved into Grove House, later Holford House, in 1830. His son John Henry became vicar of **Christ Church**. The Holfords were also involved in the Literary and Scientific Society and the Rifle Volunteers.

In 1880 Holford Road was built through the grounds of Holford House. Halas and Batchelor, makers of cartoon films such as *Animal Farm*, lived at No.6 for many years.

The Hollow Tree

Otherwise called the Great Elm, the Hollow Elm or the Great Tree. An etching by Hollar dated 1653 and printed in Park's history shows an enormous elm tree surmounted by an octagonal wooden structure reached by a winding staircase of forty-two steps within the hollow. The tower was 34 ft in circumference, and said to be capable of holding twenty persons; there were seats for six. The view was much praised by contemporary poets such as Robert Codrington. The shade of the tree attracted Puritan preachers and the tower allegedly contained a Dissenters' school for twelve young gentlemen.

J J Park had not determined its situation, but grants of land in the Manor Rolls and Sun insurance records reveal that it was near the southern tip of **Hampstead Green**. In 1709 William Kent was granted part of the verge "near the Great

The renowned Hollow Tree, after an etching by Wenceslaus Hollar, 1653. It was an elm, believed to have been located on Hampstead Green near today's Royal Free Hospital.

Elm" and by 1715 had built a pub there, initially called the Great Tree but by then called the George. Perhaps even then the Tree had been pulled down.

Holly Hill and Holly Bush Hill

Holly Hill follows an ancient track that until the 19th century took most of the traffic through Hampstead en route to Hendon, as can be seen in Rocque's map of 1746. In the 18th century it was also called Cloth Hill which suggests that some of the many local laundresses were hanging out their washing on the holly bushes that lined the west side until the 1940s. It is now steep and canyon-like, much lowered over the years by digging from surrounding sandpits.

Key buildings include the University College Junior School on the site of Holly Hill House, **Romney's House** and behind the small green on Holly Bush Hill a group of Listed early 18th-century houses. They mark the start of Windmill Hill named from the two **windmills** that crowned the hill here in the early 17th century. Bolton House was built in 1735, and home for many years of Joanna Baillie (1762-1851), a popular dramatist of her day who was much visited by the Romantic poets and especially by Sir Walter Scott, who thought her the best dramatic writer since Shakespeare. She was among the first women to be commemorated with an official plaque.

Holly Place

One of the most picturesque groups of buildings in Hampstead, which include **St Mary's Roman Catholic Church** in the middle of a terrace of houses. On the corner, No.9 has a Hampstead plaque to show that this was the Watch House for the new police force from 1830. Composer Sir William Walton (1902-83) was living next door at No.10 from 1935 to 1948, when he wrote the film score for Laurence Olivier's *Henry V*. At right angles to Holly Place are the curious weather-boarded semis of Prospect Place (the view is over the churchyard extension), traditionally built by French refugees. They certainly block the prospect from neighbouring Benham's Place.

Holly Bush Hill, 1937. Watercolour by I. Sheldon-Williams.

Holly Place, probably pre-First World War, with St Mary's church to the left. Painting by Dorothy Whitburn.

Horse Racing

An 18th-century phenomenon in Hampstead. On 3 October 1723 notice was given of a race at Hampstead **Wells** of Galloway horses, with a carthorse race the following day. However, the West Heath became the site of the Hampstead racecourse, on then flat ground behind **Jack Straw's Castle**. In 1733 a three-day August meeting was advertised, each race to consist of several circuits around 'the mile course'. The great Nonconformist preacher, George Whitefield, wrote in his diary in 1739 that he took his station under a tree near the horse-course at Hampstead. He was preaching there by invitation, and his audience, he tells us, were "some of the politer sort ... most were attentive, but others mocked".

J J Park recorded that the races "drew together so much low company, that they were put down on account of the mischief that resulted from them." This occurred some time

after 1748. As late as 1853 a road across the top of the Heath was a 'race ground' on Sundays, but the reference must be not to horses but **donkeys**.

Hospitals

Hampstead's most prominent hospital in every sense is the Royal Free – a stark reminder of the institutional architecture of the 1970s. It stands on the site of the Fever Hospital, which began in a camp of temporary wooden and corrugated iron huts with 90 beds, built on the Bartrams estate by the Metropolitan Asylums Board which had bought the land in 1868. The hospital survived until 1872, unlike some of the local inhabitants, who were fatally infected by smallpox. This danger was the main objection made to the proposed building of a bigger and better North Western Fever Hospital here in 1874. It was delayed by many powerful opponents, including Sir Rowland Hill, who lived in adjoining Bartrams House. In 1883 the Board agreed to buy Bartrams

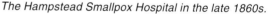

The Hampstead Smallpox Hospital in the late 1860s.

ESCAPE OF A PATIENT FROM THE HAMPSTEAD HOSPITAL

The lurid Illustrated Police News *in 1871 reported on scandalous happenings, leading to an offical enquiry, at the Hampstead Smallpox Hospital. It was alleged that dead bodies were left lying in their beds in the ward overnight, and others said that nurses tied delirious patients to their beds with sheets, causing sores and wounds as they tried to release themselves. It was recounted how one patient got free of his ties and tried to escape through a window - a scene imaginatively depicted above complete with a policeman and dogs.*

and three acres from Sir Rowland's son and move the hospital's entrance from Haverstock Hill to Fleet Road. Bartrams House was used as a nurses' home and committee rooms and the hospital was rebuilt with larger pavilions. In 1948 it became the north western branch of the Royal Free teaching hospital group, with about 275 beds. Infectious cases were transferred to Coppetts Wood hospital, Hornsey.

Plans to replace the Royal Free Hospital, Gray's Inn Road, with a new building on the site of the North Western Fever Hospital began in 1954 but only in 1968 did work begin on the building to replace the Royal Free's many scattered units. The new teaching hospital, on a fifteen-acre site, was designed by Alexander Gray, and the main structure was a cruciform tower of eighteen storeys. It was opened in 1974 with 871 beds and became fully operational in 1975. The hospital was officially opened by Queen Elizabeth in 1978, 150 years after the hospital's foundation.

Hampstead General Hospital was founded in 1882 by Dr W Heath Strange as Hampstead Home Hospital and Nursing Institute in a house in Parliament Hill Road, initially taking paying patients only. In 1901 a site facing Hampstead Green was obtained for a general hospital and Bartrams House purchased from the Fever Hospital. The house was demolished and a new building was opened on the site in 1905. In 1907 another voluntary hospital the North West London in Camden Town, amalgamated with the Hampstead General. Local doctors objected because they felt most local residents could pay for medical attendance rather than attend the enlarged hospital. The later removal to Hampstead of the Royal Free, led to the replacement of Hampstead General. The hospital building was demolished and the site used for a car park and a small garden dedicated to Heath Strange.

Other hospitals have included the New End hospital, begun during World War One in the workhouse and infirmary buildings as a convalescent home for

Hampstead General Hospital photographed prior to demolition. Its site is now covered by the car park of the Royal Free Hospital.

wounded soldiers. In 1930 the London County Council took over the running of it, and in 1948 it became part of the NHS system. When the new Royal Free opened, New End was retained as a geriatric hospital but was closed in 1985. The site was sold to Berkeley Homes who converted the hospital buildings for residential use.

The North London (later Mount Vernon) Hospital for Consumption and Diseases of the Chest was founded in 1860 in Fitzroy Square. Its chateau-like building in Mount Vernon was designed by Roger Smith in 1880, and much enlarged over the years. In 1904 a new Mount Vernon hospital was opened at Northwood, where by 1913 it was decided to concentrate its work. The Hampstead building was taken over until 1980 by the National Institute for Medical Research. Among its directors living there was physiologist Sir Henry Dale, now commemorated with a blue plaque. The National Institute for Biological Standards and Control was subsequently based here, but the building has now been converted into apartments.

Mount Vernon Hospital in Northwood took over the work of another Hampstead hospital in 1967, when the Marie Curie hospital, founded in 1929 for women cancer patients, then at No.66 Fitzjohn's Avenue, was closed because the accommodation was unsuited to new developments in radiotherapy.

The Hampstead Children's Hospital, founded in 1875, moved to Northcourt, No.30 College Crescent by 1907. In 1948 it became part of the Royal Free group and the children were treated elsewhere; the building itself became the Royal Free's preliminary training school. The Royal Free also took over the Queen Mary's Maternity Home in 1972, closing it within a few years. It had been founded by the queen for the wives of servicemen and opened in 1919 in temporary premises at Cedar Lawn, North End Road, provided by Lord Leverhulme. He also gave the site for the permanent building at Upper Heath, formerly the Upper Flask, which opened in 1922. The queen made frequent visits, donating her own crochet-work for the cots. St Columba's hospital or home of peace was founded in Islington in 1885 as the Friedenheim hospital. It was intended for poor people in the last stages of acute disease. It moved in 1892 to Sunnyside at Swiss Cottage. In 1915 the name was changed to St Columba's. In 1957 it moved to The Elms, Spaniard's Road, where it had 35 beds, but closed in 1981.

Leigh Hunt

In 1812 the poet and critic Leigh Hunt (1784-1859), living in a cottage in West End, published an attack on the Prince Regent, for which he was found guilty of libel and spent two years in prison. The libel made him hugely popular but prison damaged his health and to recuperate in spring 1816 he went to live in the **Vale of Health**. His fame followed him and his literary circle increased. His home became the centre for most of the leading literary figures of the day, including Byron and Shelley, who were supposed to have shared a cottage in the Vale, where they inscribed lines on a window. Shelley entertained

Leigh Hunt in 1810.

Hunt's many children by sailing paper boats on the pond. The Vale, with its modest but picturesque cottages surrounded by the Heath, was the perfect setting for the Romantic poets, and Leigh Hunt's circle was important in establishing the literary and politically radical tradition later associated with Hampstead. Leigh Hunt moved away in 1819 but returned in 1820 to remain until he joined the migration of poets to Italy in 1821.

Leigh Hunt's cottage has not been definitely identified. Although he called it 'little', Leigh Hunt gave musical evenings there and it housed his wife and five children. Walford claimed it was on the site of South Villa, which today boasts a home-made plaque. Helen Bentwich felt it was most likely Vale Lodge. But most of the early-19th-century cottages in the north of the Vale claim to have been the residence of the poet. Rose Cottage, which is no exception, housed the impecunious Harmsworth family from 1870-73. Here the youthful Alfred (1865-1922) and Harold (1868-1940), both later press barons, were friendly with George Jealous, editor of the *Ham & High*. He lived at

No.1 Villas-on-the-Heath and inspired Alfred, the future Lord Northcliffe, with a gift of a toy printing set. It was another editor, Ernest Rhys (1859-1946) of the Everyman Library, who while living at Rose Cottage in the 1890s changed the name to Hunt Cottage, believing it to have been Leigh Hunt's house.

Isokon

One of first domestic buildings in the world to be built with reinforced concrete, the Isokon building in Lawn Road opened in 1934. Jack Pritchard (1899-1992), who founded the Isokon plywood furniture firm, commissioned the young architect Wells Coates (1895-1958) to build the flats. He used designs by Marcel Breuer and the Bauhaus architect Walter Gropius, partly to house such refugee artists. Appropriately the building was in a Bauhaus style and the flats were almost monastically minimalist, taking up the least amount of space needed by a "rational, modern person". They were nevertheless modish and

cosmopolitan, each with an all-electric kitchen like a compact galley on a yacht, although most residents ate in the Isobar downstairs.

The Isobar was designed by Marcel Breuer who also designed the well-known Isokon 'long chair' (which can be seen at **Hampstead Museum**). The Isobar attracted a circle of artists and academics delighting in the food of Philip Harben (1906-70) (later the first TV chef), who introduced Turkish kebabs and goulash, unheard of in England in the 1930s. Residents included the Constructivist sculptors Laszló Moholy-Nagy and Naum Gabo, and the writers Nicholas Monsarrat (1910-79) and Agatha Christie (1890-1976) (it was she who compared the building's exterior to an ocean liner).

The flats were less popular post-war and the building became dilapidated. In 1968 it was bought by the *New Statesman* magazine who tore out the Isobar to make more flats and sold the block to Camden Council in 1972. For

The Isokon flats in Lawn Road.

a time demolition seemed possible, but in 2003, the building was sympathetically refurbished by Avanti Architects for Notting Hill Housing Association and is now primarily occupied by key workers under a co-ownership scheme. The refurbishment has also created a public gallery displaying reproductions of the original interiors. The block is now Listed Grade I.

There are some other notable examples of modernist buildings in Hampstead, including houses in **Frognal** and the first modernist house bought by the National Trust, No.2 Willow Road. This is part of a terrace of three built in reinforced concrete in 1938 by the Hungarian architect, Ernö Goldfinger. It replaced a row of 18th century cottages. Goldfinger's design was attacked by local preservationists — and by author Ian Fleming, who perhaps named one of his James Bond villains after the architect. This is an example of a modernist design actually lived in by its designer; most of the furniture is by Goldfinger and there are works by Henry Moore on display.

Jack Straw's Castle

Once the highest pub in London, this is now private apartments. The building's brick foundations may date to the mid 16th century, although the inn probably began in Charles II's time. In 1670 Henry Skerrett was licensed to enclose two acres of heath, by the road to Hendon, as a bowling green to entertain guests. The tavern's name was first mentioned in 1713. There was never a castle, nor is it likely that the semi-legendary rebel came here, but at the time there had been a revival of interest in Jack Straw and at least two plays were written about him. More prosaically however the name could come from a generic name for a farmworker, just as Jack Tar denoted a sailor, and Alan Farmer suggested the 'castle' was an ancient earthworks.

By the mid 18th century Jack Straw's Castle, popular both with visitors to the Wells and with travellers, was important in publicizing the attractions of the locality, with its ease of access from London, proximity to the Heath, and wide views. It was long favoured by artists and writers. They included Washington Irving and Dickens, who from 1838 often read manuscripts to his friends over dinner here. It is mentioned in Bram Stoker's *Dracula* of 1897, by which time the pub was associated with theatrical figures and many local clubs. Largely destroyed by bombing in the **World War Two**, it was rebuilt in 1962 by Raymond Erith and Quinlan Terry, in a fanciful style with

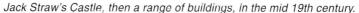

Jack Straw's Castle, then a range of buildings, in the mid 19th century.

The Hampstead Synagogue in Dennington Park Road.

Richard Seifert in 1964.

The period between the two world wars brought many Jewish refugees from Europe and several congregations set up their own synagogues, including the Regent's Park and Belsize Synagogue in Eton Villas in 1938, which was rebuilt as the South Hampstead United Synagogue in 1962.

After the war the Shomrei Hadath synagogue was opened in 1946 in the former West Hampstead Congregational church, No.527A Finchley Road. This was converted into the apartment block, The Octagon, in 1991, and the congregation moved to a smaller purpose-built synagogue adjoining it, in Burrard Road. In Belsize Square a synagogue was opened in 1947 in the former vicarage of St Peter's; the building was replaced by a modernist structure in 1958. Its basement regularly floods due to the nearby Tyburn stream.

Judges' Walk

A shaded path at the end of Windmill Hill with steps down into **Branch Hill**. It acquired its name early in the 20th century from the tradition that judges exercised here when they moved out of plague-ridden London in 1665 to hold assizes in Hampstead. This tradition was verified in the 1850s by Sir Francis Palgrave but doubters point out that nearby Branch Hill Lodge was known as Judges' Bench House. The walk affords a spectacular view over the West Heath towards Hendon and Harrow that was often painted, if not always accurately, by Constable.

weatherboarding and battlements. The pub survived until the new Millennium, but has since been turned into luxury flats.

Jews

Like other City merchants, many Jews bought houses as country retreats. Daniel Defoe commented in the 1720s that Jews seemed to have a preference for Highgate and Hampstead, but noted there was no place of worship. More widespread settlement took place from 1870, Jews following the spread of building north and west. The newcomers were served by St John's Wood synagogue, Abbey Road, just south of the parish, from 1876 until Hampstead synagogue opened in 1892 in Dennington Park Road. It was founded by among others Joseph (Lord) Duveen and designed to accommodate 700. It was built on the site of Lauriston Lodge, a large house built c.1800 by Germain Lavie and later occupied by Sir William Woods, Garter King of Arms, reputedly the last person to be buried inside the parish church. The synagogue now includes a Community Centre added by

Judges Walk is on the right, and Capo di Monte, in Windmill Hill, is to the left. Watercolour by A R Quinton, 1910.

John Keats

During his short life John Keats was closely associated with Hampstead. He was born in London in 1795 but details of his birth are obscure; his father certainly owned property and was not an ostler as some 19th-century biographers claimed. At fourteen he was apprenticed to the surgeon and apothecary Thomas Hammond in Edmonton, but at some time, probably in 1813, Keats quarrelled with him and moved out, perhaps to live with his brothers in St Pancras. He gave up the medical profession to write. In 1817, when he had come into some money, he and his brothers looked for lodgings in Hampstead. **Leigh Hunt** was living in the **Vale of Health** and his cottage there was a meeting place of up-and-coming young writers and artists.

Keats found No.1 **Well Walk**, adjacent to the Green Man, both now covered by Wells Tavern. At his lodgings John wrote *Endymion* – a thing of beauty is a joy forever – and nursed his consumptive brother Tom until he died in December 1818. This act of fraternal devotion may have hastened the development of the same fatal disease in himself, although both his mother and uncle also died of tuberculosis.

In February 1816 the antiquary and critic Charles Wentworth Dilke and a retired St Petersburg merchant Charles Armitage Brown had built for themselves a pair of semi-detached houses called Wentworth Place, in the newly emerging district of **Downshire Hill**. Brown was a good friend of Keats and after Tom's death

invited him to share his house at Wentworth Place. Soon afterwards Dilke let his semi to the Brawne family, who moved there in April 1819. During spring and summer 1819 Keats lived next door to Fanny Brawne, whom he came to love. This was his most creative period. The garden's birdsong inspired his best-known poem, *Ode to a Nightingale* and the spot where he wrote it is marked in the garden.

In 1820 Brown let Wentworth Place for the summer, so Keats took lodgings in Kentish Town, to be near to Leigh Hunt. A serious attack of blood-spitting in June obliged him to move into Hunt's house. After mid-July he was too ill to write. He moved out in August to live with the Brawnes in Wentworth Place for the month leading up to his departure for

Keats House c. 1906.

Italy, where his doctors had advised him to go for his health. Keats saw Fanny for the last time in September, when he sailed to Italy. He died in Rome on 23 February 1821, and was buried three days later in the Protestant cemetery there.

In 1896 a brown plaque to Keats was erected on Wentworth Place (by then converted into one house) by the Royal Society of Arts, and in 1920-21 the house was rescued from demolition by public subscriptions, largely from America. From 1925 it was opened to the public as Keats House. It is now run by the City of London. The house abounds with relics and contains an ever-increasing collection, including first editions and letters, a lock of Fanny Brawne's hair in a glass case and a painting of Keats by Joseph Severn. A thorough restoration of the house took place in 2009.

Kidderpore Hall

A stuccoed Greek Revival house, built in 1843 by architect T Howard for John Teil, an East India merchant with tanneries in the Kidderpore district of Calcutta, who lived here until his death in 1853. The house survives at the top of the hill in Kidderpore Avenue, which was laid out over its long carriage drive in 1890, when Westfield College acquired 2.5 acres of the estate. Part of the estate had been sold in 1856 to the West Middlesex Water Company, who had built Kidderpore Reservoir.

Westfield College originated in Maresfield Gardens in 1882, founded for the higher education of women but based on Christian principles, the Girton of North London. It

The architect's plan for an idyllic development of the Kidderpore Hall estate.

made considerable additions to the house before eventually moving to East London in 1992. Many of the buildings around Kidderpore Hall are now used by King's College as a student village.

Opposite at Nos.19-21 Kidderpore Avenue is the Hampstead School of Art, founded in the 1960s under the aegis of the Hampstead Artists' Council, initially at the Camden Arts Centre. Practising artists teach a whole range of the fine and applied arts to all age groups.

Just down the hill is the impressive Arts and Crafts church of St Luke's, Kidderpore Avenue, completed in 1899 and designed by Basil Champneys, who also built the vicarage at No.12.

Kilburn

A district on both sides of the Kilburn High Road which forms the boundary between Camden and Brent. Kilburn was until recently a heartland of London's Irish community although Irish people make up fewer than 10% of the population today.

Itsname derives from the stream that rose by West End. The stream has long since disappeared from view, having been arched over, and made to do duty as a sewer. In about 1134 it was called Cuneburna, the royal or possibly cow's stream; others have held it to mean 'cold water', the kyle-bourne. The name was also applied to **Kilburn Priory** built beside the stream, which here joined another, the Westbourne on its way to the Thames at Chelsea via the Serpentine in Hyde Park.

By 1646 there were at least ten houses and five cottages in Kilburn and the settlement grew as a minor halt on the London to St Albans road, with inns to serve travellers. In 1714 a medicinal well was discovered and exploited near the Bell inn, which opened **Kilburn Wells** to imitate those in Hampstead, but unlike Hampstead, this did not stimulate building.

There were abortive attempts at development in the early 1820s on the **Greville estate**; building resumed there from the 1840s. There was little building elsewhere in Kilburn before 1860, when the Hampstead Junction Railway was built across the Gilberts estate. The estate was bought by land companies and streets such as Iverson Road laid out from 1869. Adjoining it to the south was the Little estate, where Donald Nicoll built Palmerston Road in 1865. The Powell-Cottons owned much land in Kilburn which was not developed until the later Victorian period: lands east of **Shoot-up Hill** were built up from the 1880s and on the western side of West End Lane, on the former Liddell estate, in the late 1890s after the Chimes, a large house of the 1860s was demolished.

In Quex Road the massive Catholic Church of the Sacred Heart was founded by the Oblates of Mary Immaculate in 1866 and begun the next year. The priests were able to hear confession in the native Gaelic of the first Irish settlers in the area. They also hoped to attract non-Catholics and the church expanded rapidly and probably helped to encourage more Irish to Kilburn.

By the early 20th century building in Kilburn was mainly complete. Most houses were terraced and, by Hampstead standards, densely packed, but even so rising population and rising rents led to the division of houses among families and the taking of lodgers. Charles Booth in his researches into class and poverty in London had noted the overcrowded squalor of the whole area and the arrival of immigrants, especially the Irish, whose numbers increased further in the inter-war period. In the 1930s most of the larger houses were replaced by flats. Kilburn had by then become a popular place for public entertainment and entrepreneurs established several variety theatres and cinemas.

Bomb-damage was wide-spread during **World War Two**. Extensive rebuilding included several large council estates such as Kilburn Gate, Templar House and in the 1970s Webheath. Nevertheless traces of Kilburn's history can be found: in the pubs on the High Road which though rebuilt still stand on their original sites and certain houses on the **Greville estate** surviving from the earliest phase of development.

From the 1960s Irish immigrants have been joined by those from the Commonwealth and elsewhere and today Kilburn is a cosmopolitan area.

Kilburn Empire

The New Empire Theatre of Varieties was opened in 1907 at Nos.9-11 The Parade, as a music hall and circus. It was an ornate, three-storey building, which seated nearly two thousand and had a stage equipped with animal traps and pits. It attracted stars such as Marie Lloyd, George Robey and Houdini. Films were also

The road to Hampstead as seen from Kilburn. This 19th-century view shows the bridge over the river Kilbourne and the tower of St John, Hampstead.

shown but live acts predominated in the 1920s, when it became the Kilburn Empire. In 1949 it was converted to a modern cinema and renamed The Essoldo. This cinema survived, with a change of name, until 1971, when the exterior was clad in sheet metal and inside the auditorium was built a small cinema, which closed for good ten years later. The whole building was demolished in the 1990s and replaced by a large hotel opened in 1996, now the London Marriott Hotel, Maida Vale.

Kilburn High Road

Part of the ancient Watling Street, later the Edgware Road, there were few buildings here before the 19th century. The oldest was probably the Red Lion, which bears a plaque recording its establishment in 1444, when it stood close to **Kilburn Priory**; it was rebuilt most recently in 1890. The Old Bell is housed in a building dating from 1863, but has been on this site since about 1600. In its grounds **Kilburn Wells** was developed from 1714. The Black Lion may have started in 1666; it was rebuilt in a flamboyant Flemish style in 1898.

Before Kilburn was built up in Victorian times the High Road was lined with farms and a handful of large houses. The stateliest home was The Grange, which first appears in rate books in 1833; Nos.234-6 mark the site. The house was built by Samuel Ware, architect to the Duke of Portland, and was pulled down in 1910, although at the auction it was claimed to have been the residence of Catherine of Aragon. Its grounds became Kilburn Grange park, a popular

The Grange off Kilburn High Road. Its site is now covered by Nos. 234-236 and its grounds are now Kilburn Grange Park on the east side of the road.

open space. North of present Gascony Avenue stood Clarence House, where the young Thomas Hardy lodged in 1861-62, when an assistant to the architect (Sir) Arthur Blomfield. He later asked Hardy to supervise the evacuation of graves when the Midland Railway cut through St Pancras churchyard, an experience that had a profound effect on the young man: he gave up architecture and returned to his native Wessex to take up the pen.

Kilburn High Road has been a major shopping centre since about 1870 (see **Shops**) but it has also been home to several variety theatres, such as the **Kilburn Empire** and **cinemas**. Today the main cultural landmark of Kilburn is the Tricycle Theatre but that lies in Brent.

In the 1990s Kilburn High Road was named the 'Music Mile' by the London Tourist Board, with Irish and country music the main specialities. Sinead O'Connor performed at the Kilburn Empire. Nearly all these establishments have gone and the Music Mile is no more, although several pubs still have an Irish flavour.

Kilburn Priory

This stood roughly where the present Belsize Road meets Kilburn High Road, but its last traces had disappeared by the early 19th century.

Some time in the 12th century a hermit called Godwyn who lived on the banks of the Kilburn stream, gave his cell into the hands of Abbot Herbert of Westminster, who founded a Benedictine nunnery there around 1134. Godwyn was appointed master and warden for life and the first three nuns were Emma, Gunhild and Christina, supposedly maids of honour to Henry I's queen, Matilda. The priory was always a small establishment, with a prioress and four to six nuns, usually daughters of wealthy men in the City. Though dignified with the name of priory, it was never an important religious house. The whole building, beside the church, contained only twelve rooms.

Attached to the priory was a *hostium* where the nuns were obliged to give a free night's board and lodging to anyone travelling the road. By the 14th century, after the dense forest in this area was cut down, the road was safe enough to

The alleged remains of Kilburn Priory being used as farm buildings. Date unknown.

become the chief pilgrim route to St Albans and the traffic became a real burden to the nuns. Travellers tended to congregate at the Priory before ascending **Shoot-up Hill**, waiting to form groups for protection against robbers. Additional revenue had to be provided to the Priory by the Abbot of Westminster.

Dissolved in 1536 and swapped by King Henry VIII for the manor at Paris Garden in Southwark, it was subsequently owned by a variety of families. In 1773 Richard Middleton of Chirk Castle owned the land and divided it in two – the Shoot-up Hill estate, sold to John Powell of Fulham, and the Abbey Farm estate.

An engraving of the slight remains of the Abbey at this period was published by J J Park in 1814 but by then they had been destroyed.

In 1850 railway works unearthed tiled flooring and human bones. Also found a few years later was a tiny brass plate thought to depict a 14th-century prioress; it is preserved in St Mary's church, Priory Road.

Kilburn Tollgate

In 1710 the state of the Edgware Road was so ruinous that an Act of Parliament was passed to set up a Turnpike Trust in the hope of improving it. As building spread up the road the tollgates were moved progressively northward. The Kilburn gate stood roughly where Kilburn High Road takes over from **Maida Vale**. Vehicles were charged one penny a wheel and cattle at one farthing per head. Church traffic for weddings and funerals was exempt. The gate was removed to Willesden Lane in 1864, where it stood until the early 1880s, just before local authorities were made responsible the road.

Kilburn Wells

A spring of fresh water near the site of **Kilburn Priory** may have been one of the so-called holy wells with which the vicinity of London abounded in Catholic times. From 1714 it was exploited by the neighbouring Bell Inn as Kilburn Wells, in emulation of Hampstead Wells. The water was mildly chalybeate and promoted as medicinal. In 1801 Dr John Bliss analysed it and found that it left a salty taste and had a distinct, rather foul odour when agitated. Its purgative effect, surprisingly, was slow and gentle.

A Great Room on Kilburn High Road was advertised as being particularly adapted for "the amusement of the politest companies" and the Bell charged 3d. a glass for the water.

The pleasures of the area were promoted in *Stanzas on Kilburn Wells and its Situation* by 'T S', which began

The tollgate which straddled Kilburn High Road was removed in 1864.

Where sweet sequester'd scenes inspire delight,
And simple Nature joins with ev'ry art,
At KILBURN WELLS their various charms unite,
And gladly all conspire to please the heart.

The tea gardens in the grounds, opened by 1733, attracted thousands of visitors, many coming from London on foot. The *Public Advertiser* of 17 July 1773 noted the gardens had been "enlarged and greatly improved…fit either for music, dancing, or entertainments". Some of the latter were not particularly edifying: dog-fights and pugilistic encounters were common. There were duels too, a famous one being between Benedict Arnold, notorious as a traitor to the Americans, and the Earl of Lauderdale in 1792. But there were also theatrical perform-ances, advertised as late as 1821, when a poster added "roads well watched and lighted".

The water was publicised until about 1841, but the Old Bell (or Kilburn Wells) was still popular as a tea garden, with a music hall, for some years after that. In 1863 the old pub was replaced by the present building.

The exact location of the spring has been disputed. A plaque at No.42 Kilburn High Road claimed it as the site but Colloms and Weindling believe it was behind the shops on the High Road fifty metres north of Belsize Road.

Kingswell

The name of an estate, a well and a shopping precinct.

By 1312 Robert de Kynges-well is recorded as a free tenant of the Hampstead manor, who was nonetheless obliged to provide the lord annually with two geese and a fowl. His estate consisted of a house and sixteen acres. A farmhouse built on its northern boundary was replaced when **Church Row** was begun in the early

18th century. A barn was then built next to the lane which became **Fitzjohn's Avenue**. Called Mount Farm by 1870 it disappeared in the subsequent development of the area.

The original King's well stood roughly at the junction of High Street and Heath Street, marked on a map of Hampstead Heath of 1680. In the 15th century the High Street was known as Kingswell Street which suggests the well was then the main source of water. By the 1750s it had been built over.

The name was revived in the 20th century by the promoters of a new development in Heath Street, close to the old well. Advertised as 'a new shopping concept', it was designed by Ted Levy, Benjamin and Partners and opened in 1972. Unrepentantly modernist, angular and curving four-storey concrete buildings clad in white enclosed a piazza. By the 1980s there was a very high turnover among the retailers and the new owners used a different architect to revamp the whole in 1984, and raised rents. By the early 1990s many units lay empty. New developers claimed that it had become impossible to let the vacant units even to charity shops at zero rent and that the piazza was full of undesirables. After a planning appeal, a complete redesign of Kingswell went ahead and a continuous glazed façade along the street was erected. The shopping centre was reopened in 1995.

Leg of Mutton Pond

This pond on West Heath was probably dammed as part of a post-Waterloo plan to employ the poor; the adjoining roadway was made by some parish paupers in 1825. E Arnot Robertson said the pond was named not because of its shape but after a local resident had thrown a leg of mutton in it one warm summer's day and left it

Stanfield House, the Hampstead Subscription Library, 1910.

there to prove that the water was pure. When he eventually pulled it out, he cooked and ate it without ill-effect. The pond was marked simply as a reservoir in 1891, although already known by its modern name. In 1976 members of the Hendon and District Archaeological Society unearthed Mesolithic material dating back to around 7000 BC.

Libraries

Legislation in 1850 empowered local authorities to levy a halfpenny rate to fund public libraries and museums, but no action was taken in Hampstead until the 1890s. The town already had its own subscription library of general literature and elementary science opened in 1833 at No.65 Flask Walk. It was called Hampstead Public Library, and **Constable** and Joanna Baillie had both been founder members. Support declined in the 1840s with competition from the circulating libraries, but a new committee introduced graduated subscriptions and leased **Stanfield House** in 1885, a property now part of Nos.85-89 **High Street** at the corner with Prince Arthur Road. Free lending to working-class readers started two years later at what was by then called Hampstead Subscription Library. It survived at Stanfield

The first Hampstead Central Library, in Arkwright Road, built in 1897 and pictured here c. 1905. It now houses the Camden Arts Centre.

West Hampstead Library at the corner of Westbere and Sarre roads. It was destroyed by bombing in 1940.

House until 1966, when Christian Scientists took over the building.

The first public library to be opened was a temporary one at No.48 Priory Road, Kilburn in 1894, which included lending and reference libraries and a reading room. It was followed by the Belsize Branch library in Antrim Road three years later; its building was replaced in 1937. The Central Library, at the corner of Finchley and Arkwright roads, was also opened in 1897, the cost covered by a gift from **Sir Henry Harben**. Its reference library housed 8,000 volumes formerly owned by Professor Henry Morley, bought by the Vestry in 1896, and a local archive collection was begun. It was extended in 1909 to include a children's library, one of the first of its kind in London. The library closed in 1964 and the building became the **Camden Arts Centre**. The Central Library was then transferred to the new Swiss Cottage library at the **Swiss Cottage Centre**, an oval-planned building designed by Sir Basil Spence. This was opened by the Queen in 1964. The library also housed much of Camden borough's local history collection and

archives (subsequently moved in the mid 1990s to Holborn Library). At the same time Spence designed the adjacent swimming pool and sports centre, which was found to be unsatisfactory over the years and has since been replaced.

West End, later West Hampstead, branch library was opened in 1901 at the corner of Westbere and Sarre roads. The building was destroyed by bombing in 1940. After using temporary premises, a new branch library was built at the corner of Dennington Park Road and West End Lane in 1954. In 1931 a new Heath branch library was opened in the grounds of Keats House to serve also as a museum for the **Keats** collection formed by Sir Charles Dilke and given to the borough in 1911. A new state-of-the-art library, designed by Alan Power was opened in April 2006 at Nos.12-22 Kilburn High Road. It includes a youth centre and a community garden.

Littleworth

Small plots were taken from the Heath near **Jack Straw's Castle** in the 1720s and 1730s and a hamlet of humble cottages

grew up. It included two parish poor houses. The gentry felt the settlement was indeed of little worth and it was swept away to be replaced by villas set in extensive grounds, and the area lost its former name, often being called simply the Heath. This was after Francis Willes bought up many plots, including the poor houses, and acquired grants of waste to make a total of over two acres centred on his house, later called Heathlands. He was knighted for secret service work as a Decipherer, a position that his family monopolised for 125 years.

In 1775 the actress Mrs Lessingham (1739-83) was granted two acres of waste west of the road to North End, where she began erecting a house. The excavations were filled in by protestors who said that as she was not a copyholder she was not entitled to the grant. In 1776 she overcame the technicality by buying a cottage at Littleworth and succeeded in building Heath Lodge, a three-

The actress Mrs Lessingham in the costume of Oriana (Queen Elizabeth I) in 1777.

storeyed house designed by James Wyatt. Its grounds now form part of the Hill Garden.

Near to Heath Lodge was **The Hill**, home from 1807 of Samuel Hoare the younger. Two adjacent cottages behind Jack Straw's Castle came to be occupied by John, after 1806 Baron, Crewe. At what became Crewe Cottage, his wife Frances Crewe, the celebrated beauty and Whig hostess, entertained Fox, Burke, Sheridan, Reynolds, Canning and Fanny Burney. Her interests included helping refugees from the French revolution, quite a few of whom were attracted to Hampstead. Camelford Cottage was home in 1807 to William Wyndham, Baron Grenville, when he led the government which abolished the slave trade. By 1890 Sir Richard Temple had built Heath Brow on the site of Crewe Cottage.

The villas, which grew to prestigious size, were mostly destroyed by a parachute mine in 1941 and their grounds were added to the Heath in 1952.

Load of Hay

Once a picturesque wooden inn, called the Cart and Horses, it was first mentioned in licensing records as the Load of Hay in 1721, although the earlier name was still being used on maps in 1801. The pub was a staging post before the long haul up **Haverstock Hill** and its tea-garden used to be a favourite resort of visitors on their way to Hampstead Heath. The entrance to the gardens was guarded by two painted grenadiers—flat boards cut into shape and painted.

Its most celebrated landlord was Joe Davis (d.1806). A huge man, his drunken antics and

eccentrically splendid clothes provided a great attraction. In his *Tales of a Traveller*, Washington Irving, who stayed at **Steele's Cottage** opposite in 1824, described the Irish haymakers and the drovers and teamsters who frequented the pub. In 1854 the inn was modernised and in 1863, shorn of most of its garden, rebuilt.

A gymnasium at the back (favoured by boxers Henry Cooper and Muhammad Ali) suggested its brief renaming in the 1960s as The Noble Art. It currently sports the anodyne name of The Hill, but "Load of Hay" is permanently inscribed in the pediment aloft.

Local Government

In medieval times Hampstead was controlled by the Lord of the Manor with a court held by the bailiff of Westminster, a monk. After the manor passed into lay hands the court was not leased with the rest of the manor but was reserved to the Lord, whose steward, by the mid 18th century or earlier, was usually a London lawyer. The court was then often held at **Jack Straw's Castle** and by the 19th century the main court, if not held at the inn, adjourned there for lunch. Courts were mainly concerned with land transactions. There do not appear to have been courts for Belsize and there were none for Chalcots.

From the 17th century the parish replaced the manor as the main unit of local government, with the two churchwardens as its principal officers. Meetings were usually held in the church and attended by the parish officers and other inhabitants, seventeen at most. Meetings were held quarterly in the 18th century and monthly

by the next, by then at the workhouse. In the 18th century over 90 per cent of the rate was spent directly on the poor but this had contracted to 42 per cent by 1835 as more was spent on salaries, the police, and other expenses.

The Vestry and its officers were drawn mainly from farmers, tradesmen, and especially innkeepers. Many of the principal inhabitants did not attend, preferring instead the **Hampstead Dinner Club**. The Vestry's automatic response to any problem was to appoint a committee and as Hampstead grew, it failed to govern. Speculators ran up terraces across fields with impunity, free of checks, while the Vestry passively notched up the increased income from rates.

Under the Metropolis Management Act of 1855, the old open Vestry was replaced by a restricted Vestry of 33 members elected by house-holders occupying houses rated at more than £40 a year. The Vestry met at the board room of the guardians in the **Workhouse** until 1878 when **Hampstead Town Hall** was built in Haverstock Hill. Thereafter the Vestry met more frequently, with numerous standing committees to cover its expanding activity encompassing baths and washhouses, libraries and the supply of electricity.

In 1888 Hampstead became part of London within the LCC and thereafter gentlemen and professional men became prominent, although they were drawn from areas like Belsize rather than Hampstead town. A leading figure was **Sir Henry Harben**, a vestryman from 1874 to 1900, when he became first mayor of Hampstead.

Hampstead was praised for its "business-like management" by "men of high character willing to serve"; party politics were little regarded. Indeed as the grand gentry left Hampstead once it became more and more urbanised, the public-spirited Vestry fostered civic loyalties that replaced the earlier social ties.

Under the London Government Act, 1899, Hampstead parish became a metropolitan borough divided into seven wards. The Borough was politically Conservative yet was one of the first in London to erect working class housing. Park Dwellings in Garnett Road was built in 1905-06. This was on a modest scale but its housing activity greatly increased after the Second World War, with many blocks particularly in the south and west.

In 1965 Hampstead, much against its will, was combined with St Pancras and Holborn in the new London Borough of Camden.

Lyndhurst Hall

A former Congregational church in Lyndhurst Road. The church originated in services held in an iron building in Willoughby Road until this massive hexagonal building of purple Luton bricks was erected in 1884 despite a clause, common to most Hampstead development agreements, prohibiting the construction of any dissenting chapel. It was designed by Alfred Waterhouse (1830-1905), also responsible for the Natural History Museum, and who is honoured in the adjoining Waterhouse Close, council housing for the elderly. The first Minister was the dynamic Robert F Horton, who

stayed for nearly 50 years and successfully attracted large audiences and national attention to the church. It closed in 1978 and was converted into Lyndhurst Hall.

Since 1992 this has been the home of Air Studios, a recording studio complex where many recent film and rock and pop albums have been recorded. AIR (Associated Independent Recording) was formed by George Martin who left Abbey Road studios in 1965 after producing the Beatles' early albums.

The Magdala

In a peaceful location in South Hill Park by Hampstead Heath, the pub was built in 1868 and named after Sir Robert Napier, 1st Baron Napier of Magdala (in recognition of a siege he led in Ethiopia). Outside the pub on Easter Sunday 1955 Ruth

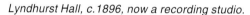

Lyndhurst Hall, c.1896, now a recording studio.

The Magdala in South Hill Park.

Ellis shot her estranged lover David Blakely who was living in nearby Tanza Road at the time. Found guilty of murder, she became the last woman to be hanged in Britain. The incident was dramatised in the 1985 film *Dance with a Stranger*. By a macabre coincidence, the second to last woman to hang, Styllon Christofi, lived in the same street and committed murder here.

Maida Vale

The northern extremity of this road, part of the ancient Edgware Road, lies in Hampstead. The first houses built were part of the **Greville Estate**, begun by George Pocock, who died at No.136, formerly No.9 Kilburn Priory. Here in 1826, Adrian-Mole like, his son John Thomas Pocock, then aged 11¾, "made up my mind to keep a daily journal of any occurrences of note". The diary has been published and gives a fascinating and moving insight into the Pococks' family life and their financial difficulties. The house was

rented by the pioneer of cinematography, William Friese-Greene, shortly before he was imprisoned for debt; it was pulled down in 1997. Vivian Court marks the former No.7 Kilburn Priory, birthplace of Leslie Hore-Belisha (1893-1957) who as Minister of Transport (1934-37) introduced pedestrian crossings marked by illuminated posts that became known as Belisha beacons. At No.138 Kilburn Fire Station opened in 1904, which was converted into the Maida Vale telephone exchange in 1922 and at No.140, now an Islamic Centre, was an early cinema the Maida Vale Palace opened in 1913, which became the first commercial bingo hall in the country.

Mansion flats

The first mansion blocks were built in the early 19th century on the Continent, providing luxurious residences for the growing urban middle class. Boasting impressive entrances, generous elevations and

balconies reminiscent of mansions, they were particularly popular in Paris. Wealthy Londoners were initially sceptical about this new style of accommodation. The idea of living in such a communal manner ran counter to dominant Victorian social ideals. Flat-dwelling was not prestigious and there were concerns about the spread of infectious diseases. By the 1880s London society by necessity had relinquished these prejudices.

More than other areas of Hampstead, West Hampstead is characterised by the emergence of the mansion flat. Whole street frontages were now given over to this form of housing. Harvard and Yale Courts, for example, occupy almost the whole length of Honeybourne Road. The flats were often large enough to accommodate at least one live-in servant.

Many mansion flats were built by the prolific Edward Cave. A particularly fine example is Marlborough Mansions, which entirely take up Cannon Hill. In 1900 Edward Cave himself lived at 38 Marlborough Mansions and his wife, Elizabeth, owned and ran the Caves' West Hampstead Estate Office from the buildings. From the start Marlborough Mansions had a high class of resident. Famous occupants include the conductor, Sir Adrian Boult (1889-1953); the novelist, Nigel Balchin (1908-70), who died here; and the painter and teacher of art, Sir William Coldstream (1908-87), who lived at Flat 87 in the 1940s.

Members of Parliament

Before 1885 Hampstead was just a part of Middlesex, although from 1681 for twenty years parliamentary elections for the county members took place on the Heath.

In 1885 Hampstead became a constituency in its own right. The election campaign was an unusual affair because it pitched a Conservative Government minister, Sir Henry Thurston Holland against a Liberal candidate who was the son-in-law of Queen Victoria, Lord Lorne, heir to the Duke of Argyll and husband of Princess Louise. Also standing was a young window cleaner, Jack Williams (Social Democrat), who had served a month in Holloway prison. He polled just 27 votes and Holland became Hampstead's first MP.

Hampstead returned Conservative MPs until the 1960s. Among them was George Balfour MP from 1918 to 1941 who founded the building firm of Balfour Beatty and Henry Brooke, MP from 1950 to 1966, who brought in the contentious Rent Act in 1956 and was Home Secretary from 1962-63. He was pilloried in *Private Eye* for his campaign against pornography and drugs. At the time he lived at No.45 Redington Road. He was ousted by Labour's Ben Whitaker, in turn replaced by the Conservative Geoffrey Finsberg (1926-96), MP from 1970 until he stood down in 1992. He lived at No.80 Westbere Road, and was created Baron Finsberg of Hampstead. He was a trustee of the **Wells and Campden Trust** for 40 years. In 1992 the Hampstead constituency was enlarged by the addition of

The old Hampstead Mortuary, now the New End Theatre.

Highgate and has been held since then for Labour by the former Oscar-winning actress Glenda Jackson.

Mortuary

In 1889 a house in **New End** was purchased as the site for a mortuary for the town, the single-storeyed building being built in 1890. It remained in use until the late 1960s. The New End Theatre opened in the building in 1974. Various play publicists and others have claimed that Karl Marx's body was laid out here prior to its interment in Highgate Cemetery. However, this could not be so since Marx died in 1883.

The Motorway Box

The shorthand name for the London Ringways network, a complex and comprehensive plan for high speed roads circling and radiating out from central London, designed to manage and control the flow of traffic within the capital. It grew out of Abercrombie's plans for London in 1943 and 1944 and was taken forward by the LCC in the 1950s, but the

fully-worked up proposal was first published by the GLC in 1966. It would have involved demolition on a massive scale and a devastating effect on Hampstead.

The North Cross Route (NCR) was the designation for the northern section of Ringway 1, the innermost circuit of the network. It would have had at least six lanes of dual carriageway. Between Kilburn High Road and West End Lane a major Y-shaped junction would have been constructed where the NCR was to meet the intended end of the M1 motorway. East of Finchley Road there were three alternative routes towards Camden Town, but the favoured one was a cut-and-cover tunnel heading south-west through Maresfield Gardens, Fitzjohn's Avenue, Belsize Park and Eton Avenue before emerging on the slopes of Primrose Hill. The GLC engineer claimed that the environment could be rebuilt over the cut-and-cover section.

The Hampstead Motorway Action Group was formed to fight the proposals, which it did tirelessly for several years, until in 1973 the GLC quietly abandoned the whole of the NCR. Most of the rest of the network was also cancelled, although the East Cross Route, part of the West Cross Route and the Westway were built.

Musicians

Many well-known musicians have lived in Hampstead.

Composers have included Sir Arnold Bax (1883-1953) at No.155 Fellows Road and Sir Arthur Bliss (1891-1975) at East Heath Lodge. Benjamin Britten (1913-76) shared a flat with his sister at West Cottages, West Hampstead when he worked with W H Auden at the GPO Film Unit. Delius once briefly borrowed Sir Henry Wood's house at No.4 Elsworthy Road; Wood (1869-1944) lived there from 1902 to 1937 and was visited by Saint-Saens, Bartok, Richard Strauss and Janacek. Sir Edward Elgar (1857-1934) moved in 1912 to the vast No.42 Netherhall Gardens, built by Norman Shaw originally for the artist Edwin Long, complete with a separate entrance for models. Elgar called it Severn House and retained it until 1921, but found it expensive to run, admitting later that he had to accept commissions for trifling theatrical works to pay for it. The house was demolished in the 1930s. No.17 King Henry's Road was the 1960s home of the prolific composer Elisabeth Lutyens (1906-83), where Alban Berg spent a few nights in 1931. Martin Shaw (1875-1958) shared rooms at No.8 Downshire Hill and Sir William Walton (1902-83) lived at No.10 Holly Place.

Apart from Wood, conductors have included Sir Adrian Boult (1889-1983) at 78

Sir Thomas Beecham.

Dame Clara Butt.

Marlborough Mansions, Cannon Hill from 1966 to 1977 and Sir Thomas Beecham (1879-1961), whose family home from 1909, purchased by his millionaire father, Sir Joseph Beecham (1848-1916), of pills fame, was at No.9 Arkwright Road. This grand house, complete with a new wing added by Sir Joseph for a picture gallery, was bought in 1921 for £10,000 by the rich railway union ASLEF and remains its HQ.

Singers have included the contralto Dame Clara Butt (1872-1936), renowned for *Abide with Me* and *Land of Hope and Glory*, at Compton Lodge, No.7 Harley Road, from her marriage in 1900 until 1929. The tenor John McCormack (1884-1945) lived before the Great War at No.24 Ferncroft Avenue and Adelina Patti (1843-1919) was at No.8 Primrose Hill Road. No.3 Oakhill Avenue was the home of the mezzo-soprano Elisabeth Schwarzkopf (1915-2006) and her husband Walter Legge (1906-79), and in 1960 the

headquarters of the Philharmonia Orchestra.

Among popular entertainers, the music hall star Marie Lloyd (1870-1922, was at.No.98 King Henry's Road in 1906. More recently, Sting lived in the 1980s, in the early years of his solo career, at No.108 Frognal, while in the 1990s Boy George was at No.18 Well Road, where he was arrested for drugs misuse. In 1997 Noel Gallagher of Oasis named his marital home at No.9 Steele's Road, Supernova Heights.

Mention should be made of Hampstead Music Club. Founded in 1946 the Club consists of about 200 singers and instrumentalists who perform both in different members' homes and in public at **Burgh House**. Since 2001 it has been an educational Charity, as it provides coaching sessions, master classes and an annual workshop led by one or more conductors of note.

New End

The original group of cottages was on the outskirts or 'end' of the town. Some of the earliest enclosures here were during the Civil War, but were not recorded. Most 17th-century building in New End was of cottages which have not survived. With the development of Hampstead as a spa at the beginning of the 18th century, an ancillary quarter sprang up here with gambling dens and souvenir shops surrounded by new homes and lodging houses. The grandest surviving property is **Burgh House**.

New End was the poor corner of Hampstead, its relatively humble cottages providing accommodation for artisans. The parish work-house was founded here in 1800 and rebuilt in 1845, serving also as an infirmary and offices for the Vestry, and later becoming New End Hospital. **Christ Church** was built in 1852 by the rich congregation of Well Walk Chapel, and the higher parts of New End became favoured by the wealthy.

Parts of New End were rebuilt in the 1930s, including the Old White Bear and the Duke of Hamilton public houses which both originated in the Wells first period. The council added a few flats after World War II and most of the shops were gradually replaced by houses. New End has lost its once lowly status.

Nonconformity

There were Puritan preachers in Hampstead before the 1660s, but Protestant dissenters came in some numbers after the 1665 Five Mile Act precluded their clergymen from preaching within five miles of London. Ralph Honywood's house on Red Lion Hill, where from 1666 he had a chaplain, was a meeting place for Presbyterians until Red Lion chapel was built close by.

The Act of Toleration of 1689 allowed dissenters to have their own place of worship. In April 1692 the manor court records the meeting place at the dwelling house of Isaack Honywood, esquire. The Honywoods were owners of an estate to the east of the High Street, originally part of the medieval Popes estate, on

New End in 1880, by J P Emslie. On the left is a former pub called the City Arms.

Carlile House, a centre of Nonconformity, stood by today's junction of Rosslyn Hill and Willoughby Road.

for Hampstead's Scottish inhabitants. Trinity Presbyterian church was begun in temporary premises in 1844, moving to the **Well Walk** chapel in 1853, and from thence to a new church built at No.2 High Street in 1862. It survived for a century until the congregation joined St Andrew's Presbyterian church erected in 1904 in Finchley Road,.

Baptists first met in Holly Bush Hill, where the Bethel Baptist chapel (later part of Holly Mount) opened in 1818. This was dissolved in 1862 after the Baptist church in Heath Street had opened. This had been founded and largely paid for by the merchant James Harvey, in gratitude for his sick son's recovery in Hampstead. The Ebenezer Strict Baptist chapel in Belsize Road was built in 1870 in memory of Thomas Creswick by his sister: he had preached nearby in the open air and the site was chosen to be near that of his last sermon.

From 1851 the Congregationalists had their own training school in College Crescent and from 1884 a huge

which they had built what became known as Carlile House (demolished in 1876). When the congregation grew, Honywood built a chapel next to his stables on this site in what was much later Willoughby Road.

Strict orthodoxy was relaxed by the 1770s and members became Unitarian. The chapel was rebuilt in 1828, but by 1862 it again proved too small, as numbers soared, and the present chapel was built on **Rosslyn Hill** by John Johnson in 1862, and enlarged in 1885. The interior was renovated in 1966 by architect Kenneth Tayler, former chairman of the congregation. Among the fine Victorian stained-glass windows are works by William Morris, Burne-Jones and Henry Holiday.

In the 1840s there was concern that there was no Presbyterian place of worship

The Unitarian Rosslyn Hill Chapel.

The Baptist church in Heath Street.

church in Lyndhurst Road, which its forceful Minister R F Horton made well-known. It is now **Lyndhurst Hall**.

George Whitefield preached on Hampstead Heath and was said to have inspired the formation of an Independent chapel, probably the Calvinistic Methodist one that met in a shed near the chapel built by 1771 at the east end of Church Row. This was pulled down in street clearances in the 1880s. A Wesleyan chapel existed on the corner of Prince Arthur Road on the site of a mansion called The Rookery, home until 1842 of the Longman publishing family, sold off in 1871. The chapel was demolished in 1935 and replaced by the 1930s blocks called Greenhill. Wesleyans also built the Methodist church in Quex Road, Kilburn on a site bought in 1868. It was replaced by 1975 by a small block of flats while the church moved to Kingsgate Road. Also in Quex Road was a Unitarian church, which opened in 1908 and closed in 1965.

Although there is a rich tradition of Nonconformity in Hampstead, it never flourished as widely among the middle-classes as it did in other parts of London. In Edwardian times Hampstead remained a bastion of the established Church.

North End

The hamlet of North End is presumed to be the Sandgate mentioned in Hampstead's charter of 986 and probably represented a gap in the surrounding woodland. From Tudor times it was often referred to as Wildwood Corner. The wood, Wildwood, was part of Eton College's

Cottages at North End, c. 1905.

Wyldes estate in Hendon, and by 1632 it marked the parish boundary. Cottages were mentioned at Wildwood Corner at the end of Charles II's reign and by 1700 the hamlet was known as North End. Ten years later there were 18 houses and cottages; the copyholders included Joseph Keble, the barrister and essayist, who came here for the air for part of the week.

There was modest growth during the early 18th century, with a few country houses appearing among the cottages, as North End was 'discovered' by Londoners. Such was the City goldsmith Robert Dingley who acquired Wildwoods, where the elder Pitt was to stay. To the east along the Sandy Road a cluster of houses were built in what was then called **Spaniard's quarter**, after the nearby inn. To the south, **Littleworth**, a hamlet of humble cottages sprang up from 1720, transformed into an area of high-class villas later in the century. The combined population for North End and Littleworth increased from 108 in 1801 to 416 by 1871.

North End was long famous for its two pubs, both of which are mentioned in the Holborn Register of 1730. The Hare and Hounds, twice bombed in 1940 and housed until the 1960s in five linked caravans, was demolished in 2001 and replaced by flats. The **Old Bull and Bush** survives. The pubs attracted many visitors in the later 19th century when most of North End was still cottages, some of whose enterprising residents had opened tea gardens.

Behind the Old Bull and Bush are some elegant houses, including Byron Cottage, named after the wealthy Lady Byron who contributed much money to the development of the Spitfire aircraft in the 1930s.

Much of North End was destroyed or damaged by a parachute mine during **World War Two**, but post-war building has generally been sympathetic to the quiet village-like atmosphere. Michael Ventris (1922-56), the architect and decipherer of Linear B, built No.19 North End Avenue in the 1950s. Sir Nikolaus Pevsner (1902-83), the architectural historian, lived from 1936 until his death in

1983 at the architecturally unremarkable No.2 Wildwood Terrace, next to Geoffrey Grigson (1905-85) the poet at No.3 in 1938. Sir Donald Wolfit (1902-68), the actor manager, lived at No.5 Wildwood Grove in the 1950s.

Old Bull and Bush

A famous pub in North End, dated traditionally from c.1645 but probably built c.1700 and first mentioned in records in 1721. There is a tradition that William Hogarth lived here when he first married but this must be apocryphal. It is also said to have been frequented by Addison and his friends, which seems more likely. Gainsborough, who drank here with Reynolds and Garrick, called it "a delightful little snuggery". Walford wrote in the 1870s that it still had pleasant tea gardens, with curiously constructed bowers and arbours.

The pub was made famous through the song *Down at the old Bull and Bush*, which dates from 1903. Quintessentially cockney? Florrie Forde, who sang it, was an Australian and the song was by a German American, Harry von Tilzer and was originally called *Under the Anheuser Busch*. The story goes that the music hall audience was having difficulty with the chorus until a boy amended it to "Down at the Old Bull and Bush (bush, bush)" and the song caught on.

The pub was reconstructed in 1924, but two 18th-century bay windows and one Venetian window were retained.

When the Hampstead Tube was first projected there was a plan for a stop at the Bull & Bush and platforms were constructed below ground, but no station was built due to local objections. Two hundred feet down, the partially built level was used for the storage of archives in the First and Second World Wars. In the 1950s it was converted into an underground control centre for 'floodgates' on the deep tubes around central London. In case these gates should ever need to be used in a war situation the control room is allegedly 'blast-protected' – even against sustained nuclear attack.

Philo-Investigists

A band of Hampstead gentlemen who (to quote Park), "setting their faces against the drinking habits prevalent in mixed society, pledged themselves to keep within the bounds of temperance, and to introduce subjects, or topics of conversation, that should tend to improve the understanding

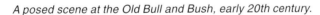

A posed scene at the Old Bull and Bush, early 20th century.

and mend the heart". Under the rather pretentious name Philo-Investigists, meaning lovers of investigation, the members held their meetings at the (Lower) Flask Tavern, where they addressed each other as "Brother Phil".

They cast medallions for themselves with Masonic-like symbols of three interlinked triangles and the motto "Brother, do all the good you can". From quarterly subscriptions and fines the Philo-Investigists established a fund for charitable purposes, setting themselves up as a benefit society. In 1787 the members, with Edward Montagu at their head, founded the Hampstead Sunday School, from which the **Hampstead Parochial School** developed.

Pilgrim's Lane

The name comes from Charles Pilgrim, who owned the neighbouring land and lived in **Vane House** on Rosslyn Hill. A plaque on No.8 with a lengthy inscription hails W J Cory who wrote the *Eton Boating Song* and died here in 1892. A master at Eton, he left the school abruptly, assumed a new surname and married a woman less than half his age. He ended his days in Hampstead, teaching classics to young ladies. For good measure, a ship's figurehead has been attached to the building.

Daniel Barenboim and Jacqueline du Pré (1945-87) made music at No.5A in their sound-proof studio during the early 1970s. Among the first residents at No.1 were the artist (Sir) William Nicholson (1872-1949) and his family. His son, the future abstract artist, Ben,

Pilgrim's Lane, 2009, showing the ship's figurehead.

attended a local school and in the 1930s returned to Hampstead to the Mall Studios in Belsize Park. In 1973 he was back in Pilgrim's Lane at No.2B, and he died there in 1982.

Pitt House

In 1727 Robert Dingley, a City goldsmith, acquired a small house set in 2½ acres in North End which was called in turn Wildwoods and North End. Politically ambitious, Dingley's son Charles invited William Pitt the elder (1708-78) to the house in 1763. He made considerable alterations, building a new wing and a gymnasium for Pitt's children by 1766, when Pitt first moved in with his wife; they fled to Bath to escape the heat two months later. Having becoming Earl of Chatham and Prime Minister, Pitt returned in 1767 but was struck down with melancholia. He retreated to an upstairs room where a hatch was built so that he could get his meals without seeing anyone. George III was so worried that at one point he threatened to visit Pitt at North End himself. Pitt left for good

in September that year, but gave his name to the house. Dingley was put up as a candidate to oppose the demagogue John Wilkes, but died in 1769 after being beaten up by the mob.

From Manor Rolls it seems that another Prime Minister, Lord North, was in possession in the early 1770s. Sir Alfred Harmsworth, younger brother of future Lord Northcliffe and himself later Viscount Rothermere bought the house in 1899. From 1914 Pitt House was the home of the Fleming family, whose famous sons, Ian and Peter, were brought up here. During the Second World War it was used by the army and then left empty until it was pulled down and replaced in 1952 by a house of the same name. A Classical archway which formed its entrance survives.

Plague

Hampstead was long noted for its healthy air, and both healthy (and unhealthy) Londoners have often been attracted to its heights. There have been many escapees from plague in the capital. The

Abbot of Westminster Simon de Barcheston fled here in 1349 to escape the Black Death, which he probably brought with him, and died in Hampstead. In the 16th century Norden commented that in times of plague citizens rushed hither. In a letter dated August 1603, Sir William Waad who lived at **Belsize** complained that the area was being invaded by Londoners escaping from the plague and dying under hedges "whereof we have experience weekeley here at Hampsted"; he wanted the refugees fined! During the Great Plague in 1665, trust in clear air on the hills brought throngs from London to Hampstead town, where in one hundred houses 260 people died.

Hampstead was spared London's cholera epidemics of 1832-33 and 1849, although Barratt records the death from the disease of an old lady who had moved to Hampstead from St Giles and insisted on drinking water from the church pump of her former parish. She never tired of praising it, but it was loaded with sewage gas and phosphates.

The old police station on Rosslyn Hill, opened in 1868. Below is its successor – itself now only partly used – built 1910-13, to the design of J Dixon Butler.

Policing

In the days of the Vestry public order was maintained, largely ineffectually, by constables. In 1707 the constables complained that they had never had the shelter of a suitable watchhouse, and the justices ordered one to be built. It was in disrepair by 1748 and its site, the roadway in Heath Street near its junction with High Street, considered very inconvenient. By 1795 the watchhouse had been moved to the bottom of Flask Walk where it stood with its two huts shortly before being demolished in 1839.

The watch could do little to prevent highway robberies and by 1774 the number of such crimes in and around Hampstead warranted a local Act for watching and lighting the town: Commissioners were empowered to raise a rate and appoint foot and horse patrols, armed if necessary. By 1828 the parish paid for a superintendent, seventeen watchmen, and eight day and night patrols.

The establishment of the metropolitan police force brought residents a large bill for building police stations. A deputation told Sir Robert Peel that the force was both oppressively expensive and unnecessary because of the local Act, to no avail. Hampstead became part of S division and a police station was opened at No.9 Holly Walk. Four years later it moved to the corner of Holly Hill and Heath Street. It was replaced in 1868 by a new station on Rosslyn Hill which in turn was succeeded in 1913 by a new station and magistrates' court at No.26½, on the corner of Downshire Hill. This is now open only in restricted hours and is closed on Sundays.

A police station for West Hampstead and Kilburn was opened at No.90 West End Lane in 1883, replaced in 1972 by one at No.21 Fortune Green Road, which houses one of London's few Mounted Police Divisions. The premises are on the site of Berridge House, opened in 1908 as part of the National Society's Training College for Teachers of Domestic Subjects and demolished in 1966.

Pond Street

There was a settlement in Pond Street by the 13th century, assisted by a plentiful supply of water. It is one of the oldest streets in Hampstead, and its name was recorded in 1607. The pond refers to the one that existed on **South End Green** at the foot of the street. The muddy pond was filled in in 1835, but until the late 1840s the name Pond Street applied not only to the road, but to the whole South End Green area. Pond Street was a hamlet surrounded by fields until the development of the **Downshire Hill triangle** from Regency times linked it to Hampstead town.

It had gained in importance as it was the route by which early carriage visitors reached the Wells, much to the disgust of traders in the High Street. Around 1800, Pond Street accommodated so many doctors it was known as the Harley Street of Hampstead. Among these were Dr Thomas Goodwin, who discovered

some local 'Neutral Saline Springs' and promoted yet another spa, and the physician Baron Dimsdale, who inoculated the Empress Catherine of Russia for smallpox. She told him to leave her country as soon as possible after the operation, as in the event of her death he would be held guilty of it.

Today doctors no longer predominate but many know Pond Street well since the street is now overshadowed by the great bulk of the **Royal Free Hospital**.

A few of the older houses survive, but Nos.23-25 were built around 1900 as the headquarters of the First Cadet Battalion of the Royal Fusiliers. Their drill hall was also used from 1908 by the 1st Hampstead Scouting troop, founded upon the recommendations of Sir Robert Baden-Powell's highly influential *Scouting for Boys* handbook which had appeared that year. They claimed to be the earliest troop in existence and were known as "The Firsts".

Near South End Green is Warwick Mansions, where George Orwell (1903-50) lodged in the 1930s. He is commemorated in a plaque on No.1 South End Road, which in 1934 was Book Lovers' Corner, and the young Orwell came to work here as a part-time shop assistant, living at the proprietor's flat in Warwick Mansions next door. Local scenes were reflected, not very favourably, in his novel *Keep the Aspidistra Flying*, published in 1936.

Leading north from Pond Street is Hampstead Hill Gardens. The earliest houses were erected by 1870, but the slightly later red-brick, Queen Anne style houses were built

Attractive groups of houses and buildings on the north side of Pond Street, including the old drill hall and the pedimented Roebuck. Opposite (not shown) is the dismal architectural contrast of the Royal Free Hospital.

mainly for prosperous artists, such as Charles Green (1840-98) at No.3. (Sir) John Summerson (1904-92), lived in No.14 in the 1930s. No.9 was home in the 1980s to the architect (Sir) Norman Foster. Aldous (1894-1963) and Maria Huxley lived at No.18 in 1919-20, their first marital home.

Potter & Sons

The iron and brass foundry of Thomas Potter & Sons was established at West End about 1860 by a local resident. It was not popular with his neighbours in what was still a mainly rural area. In 1864 he built twelve cottages immediately north of the foundry, apparently because local hostility made it impossible for his workmen to find other accommodation. There were also protests against his plans for making gas to light the workshops, with the result that a half-built gasometer could be used only as a water tank.

Among the foundry's products was metalwork. Potter & Sons supplied the outer screen walls of the Law Courts in the Strand. The foundry had closed by 1894 and was replaced by the flats called Welbeck Mansions.

Primrose Hill

The hill was on the southern boundary of Hampstead. It was so named in the reign of Elizabeth I, but there are no primroses to be seen now and the neighbouring Barrow Hill (meaning a wooded hill, not a burial mound), has been flattened to hold a reservoir. This is probably 'The Barrow', mentioned in a 10th-century document describing the boundaries of Hampstead.

In the 18th and early 19th centuries, the area round Primrose Hill and Chalk Farm became notorious as duelling grounds. In the 1830s, when cemeteries were being laid out all round London, commercial eyes were cast on Primrose Hill, and a Bill introduced in Parliament in 1837 would have allowed its enclosure. Local residents managed to persuade the Vestry to oppose the Bill. In the ensuing public agitation the Government was persuaded to secure Primrose Hill for public use. In 1842, Eton College gave up 53 acres of Primrose Hill in exchange for 32 acres of Crown land near the College.

On the open space Chartists held meetings in the 1840s and a large rally was held when Garibaldi came to London in 1864. In recent years, the hill has become the venue for Druids' rites at midsummer, while other exercises are performed in the open-air gymnasium erected in 1847, adjoining the playground.

The French Gothic basilica of St Mary the Virgin in Primrose Hill Road was designed by local architect Michael Manning. From 1901 to 1915 the vicar, Percy Dearmer, "made the church a showpiece of liturgical worship and good music", commissioning Vaughan Williams as composer for the new English Hymnal.

Pubs

Many Hampstead pubs began as beer shops selling through the front windows of their parlours. For example, the Old Black Lion in West End Lane was a licensed beerhouse in 1721 but not until the end of the 19th century was it a fully fledged tavern. It was rebuilt in 1912 and has been enlarged and modernised since.

The first inn name in Hampstead that is recorded is the King of Bohemia in 1680. It

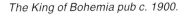

The King of Bohemia pub c. 1900.

97

was one of many inns in the High Street in the 17th century and may have originated during the period of enthusiasm for Frederick V, count palatine, James I's son-in-law, after he took the crown in 1619. Next to the pub was the entrance to the **Hampstead brewery**. Also on the east side, the White Lion was temporarily suppressed in 1641 but a "very considerable new building" had been erected on the site by 1671. The King's Head, mentioned from 1721, later called the King William IV, on the west side is probably identifiable with the Queen's Head sited on the Kinghall estate and described as much decayed in 1667.

Since Hampstead town was not on a major road from London, it lacked large hostelries for traveller, but the number of inns rose with the exploitation of the Wells and of Belsize House. The Lower Flask, in Flask Walk, rebuilt in 1873-4 as the modern Flask tavern, and the Upper Flask, in Heath Street, owed their names, if not their existence, to the exploitation of the Wells. Many 18th-century inns were resorts of Londoners. Mother Huff's tavern was recorded on the Heath, near the Elms, in 1680 and was mentioned in a play performed in 1705. On the Heath **Jack Straw's Castle** and the **Spaniard's**, both of them in 1807 "known to every citizen of London", were popular by the 1750s. However, with the decline in the Wells, by 1800 several Hampstead pubs had closed.

New inns were built to serve the 19th-century suburbs, and by 1872 there were 44 in all, including two called hotels. Tea gardens, with their multifarious amusements,

The secluded Holly Bush Tavern in Holly Mount in the 1950s.

remained popular for most of the 19th century, including those at Jack Straw's Castle, the Bell at Kilburn, the **Old Bull and Bush**, the Wells tavern and at the **Vale of Health**. Several were licensed for music and dancing and other inns had particular attractions. The Swiss Cottage tavern had a former pugilist, Frank Redmond, as its first landlord in the early 1840s and became famous as the starting point for foot races along Finchley Road.

Most of the ancient pubs were rebuilt on their original sites in the late 19th century, and some again during the next. A post war trend was to rename historic hostelries, a trend which thankfully has been reversed. For example, the historic George by Hampstead Green entered the new Millennium as the Rat & Parrot but has now regained its 18th-century name.

Quakers

Several prominent families in Hampstead, including the **Hoare** family, were at one time Quakers, yet there was no

The attractive and unassuming Quaker Meeting House in Heath Street, designed by Frederick Rowntree.

formal Meeting of the Society of Friends in Hampstead until 1897. This met in Willoughby Road until a Meeting House was built in 1907 at 120 Heath Street, designed by Fred Rowntree, later responsible for the Quaker village at Jordans in Buckinghamshire. Today this hosts a relatively large Quaker meeting, with around 50 attending on most weeks. The Resident Friend provides a Quaker presence in the local community.

Railways

The first railway in the parish was part of the main line from Euston built in 1837 by the London & Birmingham Railway Company, later part of the London and North Western Railway (LNWR). The line crossed southern Hampstead and ran beneath Primrose Hill in a much admired stone tunnel, whose turreted entrance front was designed by W H Budden. When first built, the line was merely passing through on its way to London

The Primrose Hill tunnel, 1838.

from the north. The first station on the line to serve the locality was at Kilburn, opened in 1852. The original station building survives in Belsize Road but has not been used since the 1870s. A second Hampstead station opened at the west end of the Primrose Hill tunnel, called Loudoun Road; it was closed in 1917 but reopened in 1922 as South Hampstead.

Congestion near Camden Town led the LNWR to promote the Hampstead Junction Railway (HJR) which in 1860 opened a northerly bypass to rejoin the main line at Willesden. The HJR company was absorbed by the LNWR in 1867. In the parish there were three stations along the line, whose present names are Hampstead Heath, Finchley Road & Frognal, and West Hampstead. The service was electrified in 1916 and in 1985 was rerouted to provide trains from North Woolwich to Richmond (the North London line); this is now part of London Overground.

In 1868 the Midland Railway opened its own terminus at St Pancras. Trains ran from Bedford along a line which entered the parish at Child's Hill, passed beneath the HJR's line to a second station called Finchley Road (closed in 1927) and thence through the long Belsize Tunnel towards Kentish Town. The clay dug out by hundreds of navvies provided most of the 22 million bricks needed to line the tunnel. The Midland's local service quickly proved successful, and West End (from 1905 West Hampstead) station was opened in 1871; it had previously been a halt, to serve a yard and sidings, and re-mained profitable only because of freight traffic. The buildings were demolished in 1981.

In 1865 authority was given to build a feeder line from the new underground Metro-politan line from Baker Street to Hampstead, where it was to cross High Street by a bridge and terminate at Willow Road. Financial difficulties meant

that the line never reached the town. A single track, running only as far as Swiss Cottage, was opened in 1868. Eleven years later the Metropolitan invaded the territory of the other railway companies by building a double-tracked extension to Willesden Green with stations at Finchley Road and West Hampstead. The line was electrified in 1905.

Under London Transport's new works programme of 1935, a stretch of the Bakerloo line was built in a tube beneath the Metropolitan line from Baker Street to Finchley Road, where it took over two of the Metropolitan tracks to Wembley Park and its branch to Stanmore. The new Bakerloo line opened in 1939, the Metropolitan's station at Swiss Cottage being replaced by one designed in an art deco style. After further work, the Stanmore line, renamed the Jubilee line, was inaugurated in 1979, when new entrances and a ventilation tower were built at Swiss Cottage.

Rosslyn Hill c.1905, looking south.

Hampstead town finally got its own railway station with the opening of the **Hampstead Tube** in 1907. This was the last entirely new line in central London for sixty years.

George Romney

Romney's House

A weather-boarded building (*see p. 11*) on **Holly Bush Hill**, this once belonged to the artist George Romney (1734-1802). Bred in Cumbria, he found the wide prospects of Hampstead congenial and was living part-time in the town by 1788. Eight years later he bought the stable block of a house in The Mount with a view to remodelling it into a large studio plus a spacious gallery for the display of statues and pictures. He directed the works himself, but became depressed and moved north to Kendal in 1799, returning to his neglected wife, where he died three years later. According to Barratt it all cost him £3,000, but he was able to sell the house for only £357 when he left. His son arranged the sale in 1801.

The building was subsequently enlarged for **Assembly Rooms**. In the 1880s the Liberals moved in, followed by the Constitutional Club. From 1929 until 1939 Romney's House belonged to Clough Williams-Ellis (1883-1978), architect of Portmeirion, who had it much altered, but the splendid pilastered assembly room has survived.

Rosslyn Hill

Rosslyn Hill, linking Haverstock Hill to Hampstead High Street, was first known as Red Lion Hill after an old inn. The Red Lion was demolished in 1868 and replaced by a police station, which lasted until 1913. Its site is now marked by the dried-up drinking fountain outside No.63.

In the early 19th century Red Lion Hill became Roslyn (sic) Street after the notorious Alexander Wedderburn, Earl of Rosslyn, who moved from Branch Hill Lodge to **Rosslyn House**. The road then contained a number of historic buildings such as **Chicken House** and **Vane House**. In Victorian times several places of worship were erected, **St Stephen's** on Hampstead Green, at the foot of the hill, and nearer Hampstead town, Rosslyn Hill Chapel.

Rosslyn House

This mansion, earlier known as Shelford Lodge, stood between the top of the present Lyndhurst and Wedderburn Roads. It dated back to the 16th century when it was leased by the Careys from Westminster Abbey. Howitt states that the celebrated Lord Chesterfield lived here for some years, while he held the Manor of Belsize, of which it formed a part; his ancestors might have called the house Shelford Lodge after their estate in Nottinghamshire. Shelford Lodge was leased from 1794 by the clever but unscrupulous Alexander Wedderburn (1733-1805), Lord Loughborough. This was his country retreat, standing alone amidst green fields and commanding an extensive view over the distant country. Here Loughborough used to entertain the Prince of Wales and the leaders of the Whig party, including Fox, Sheridan and Burke. He retired to Slough in 1802, and was created Earl of Rosslyn.

The house was then renamed Rosslyn House, probably by the later occupant, Robert Milligan, projector of the West India Docks, which Wedderburn had strongly supported. A West India merchant, Henry Davidson, who subsequently lived there, began developing the grounds as the Rosslyn Park Estate in the 1850s. The house had also

Rosslyn House.

been considered by Queen Victoria as a nursery for the royal children.

In 1855, after a major rebuild, Rosslyn House became an emergency shelter for seventy girls orphaned by the Crimean War. The Soldiers' Infant Home, which later became the Royal Soldiers' Daughters Home and School, originally trained the girls for domestic service. By 1858, the charity had found better premises at **Vane House** in Rosslyn Hill, and Prince Albert came in person to lead the girls up the hill to their new home.

Davidson sold Rosslyn House in 1859 to Charles Henry Woodd, who created a grand entrance in the 1860s. The gatehouse by S S Teulon partially survives. Woodd's widow sold Rosslyn House to developers in 1896, although before it came down the north side of Wedderburn Road had been begun. The comedian Barry Humphries later lived at No.4.

Rosslyn Lodge

There was a house on this site from the mid 18th century. Rosslyn Lodge was built about 1803 by Henry Cooke, a merchant then living in **Rosslyn House**. During World War One the Lodge was used as a military hospital where over 2,000 patients were treated. It was bought by the Girl Guides in 1982 and restored and extended by John Dangerfield Associates to become the headquarters of the World Association of Girl Guides and Girl Scouts, and renamed the Olave Centre after Lady Baden-Powell. Its annexe is called Pax Lodge.

Rosslyn Park Rugby Club

Founded by members of the Rosslyn Park cricket club in 1879, the club was allowed to use the grounds of **Rosslyn House** by the owner Charles Woodd; one of the first players, most of whom were teenagers, was a J Woodd. The White Horse pub was hired for a changing room and to store the goalposts and the pitch was on **South End Green** from October 1879 to March 1881 when the club moved to Gospel Oak.

Royal Free Hospital

The Free Hospital was founded by William Marsden in Hatton Garden in 1828, and revolutionised health care by offering free treatment to all. It was given the title 'Royal' by Queen Victoria in 1838, moved to Gray's Inn Road in 1840 and thence to Pond Street in 1974 and formally opened there in 1978. It has absorbed other hospitals that were founded in or moved to Hampstead – see **Hospitals**. In April 1991 the Royal Free Hampstead NHS Trust became one of the first trusts to be set up. It now has around 900 beds, employs around 4,600 people and sees about 700,000 patients a year from all over the world, with a huge range of general and specialist services. In 2009, using a legacy from a refugee from Nazi Germany, the hospital was able to give its front entrance a major facelift.

The present Royal Free buildings, which tend to blight the view from the Heath, were officially opened by the Queen in 1978. The architects were Watkins, Gray, Woodgate International.

St John's parish church

The church at Hampstead is first noted c.1244 as a chapel, part of the parish of Hendon, and also an estate of Westminster Abbey. The rector of Hendon was responsible for the cost of a separate chaplain to

The monument, in St John's churchyard, to John Harrison, the celebrated inventor of the marine chronometer which enabled mariners to determine longitude.

serve it. How and when Hampstead gained independence from Hendon is uncertain. The chapel was referred to as a parish church, and its chaplains were called parish priests, from the 1380s. In 1384 state papers record an order to set free John "the parisshe priest of Hampstede imprisoned at suit of Walter Wodewarde for rape and abduction of Maud his wife at Hampstede, his goods and chattels". Though property was described as being in Hampstead parish in 1470. Yet tithes still went to Hendon. A definite change did occur in 1478 when Westminster Abbey appropriated the chapel and became responsible for providing a chaplain at Hampstead. It was probably then that Hampstead became a separate perpetual curacy in the gift of Westminster.

After the Dissolution the right to appoint ministers fell to Hampstead's Lord of the Manor, but it was not until 1598 that the vicar (officially a

perpetual curate before 1868) was summoned to the Bishop of London's visitation and churchwardens appear. The parish registers commence in 1560.

By medieval times Hampstead's parish church was dedicated to St Mary, as was the case in Hendon. The medieval building was a quaint, irregular structure of assorted styles with steeply-pitched roofs. Constant repairs were made during the late 17th century, but by the time it was demolished in 1745, it had become unsuitable and unsafe for Hampstead's burgeoning population. In 1747 the present church was erected, dedicated simply to St John, finally identified in 1917 by the Bishop as St John the Evangelist. It was designed by a local resident John Sanderson. Contrary to all custom of the time, the belfry and tower are at the east end, probably to cut costs and to create an imposing effect at the end of **Church Row**. The

The interior of St John's parish church, c. 1857. Drawing by C J Greenwood.

church was enlarged and re-orientated in 1878, to plans by F P Cockerell (1833-78). As a result, the chancel and altar are at the west end, an unusual arrangement. The church has some fine stained glass by Clayton and Bell, and memorials to Keats and other local celebrities.

The older churchyard is romantically unstructured, attractively sloped and well wooded, and full of famous names. Twenty graves have been Listed, including those of Constable, John 'Longitude' Harrison and Norman Shaw. Many of the 17th-century burials are of nurse-children farmed out by London parents to be wet-nursed in the healthy air of Hampstead by usually unhealthy foster mothers. There is a fine collection of Georgian limestone chest tombs. In the grid-like extension to the north across the road, opened in 1812, are the tombs among many others of Sir Walter Besant, Beerbohm Tree, George du Maurier, Kay Kendall the actress, and Hugh Gaitskell, Labour leader.

The wrought iron gates and railings at the Church Row entrance to the churchyard were bought at the sale of Canons, near Edgware, in 1747.

St John's, Downshire Hill

Opened in 1823 St John's was probably intended as a chapel of ease to the parish church (hence the dedication) but was from the start a proprietary chapel, i.e. privately owned. It still is, and is the last of its kind in London. The congregation has owned the building since 2003.

St John's was the work of the builder William Woods who was responsible for much of the development of Downshire Hill. The pleasing building, with its Regency stuccoed and painted façade, includes a Doric porch and double staircased vestibule. Below the bellcote outside, the distinctive black and gold clock on the front of the building is as old as the church; made by John Moore and Son of Clerkenwell in 1823. Its simple bold design is typical of similar timepieces of that period. Inside, St John's is one of the few churches in England retaining original examples of wooden box pews.

Listed Grade I, the building has been subject to a number of restoration projects. The most recent was completed in

St John's Downshire Hill in 1912.

September 2004, when the building was underpinned and an undercroft added.

St John's Park

A small but ambitious development east of Haverstock Hill, dating to the 1860s, with handsome houses lining generous streets, laid out on the existing field lines. John Lund (d.1843), a warehouseman of Westminster, had built Haverstock Lodge in three acres of land, but in 1852 his son William exchanged the lease for a 99-year building lease and proceeded to develop the estate, which he called St John's Park. Thompson noted this was "intended to appropriate some of the allure of St John's Wood", but the name never took off. Moreover, the standing of the estate suffered from its proximity to the local Fever Hospital until smallpox patients were removed.

The service and mews area for the estate was concentrated in close-packed terraced housing in the Fleet valley, well out of sight. Downside Crescent was built on the line of the drive to John Lund's old house. The eminent war correspondent Henry Woodd Nevinson (1851-1941), known as 'the Grand Duke', lived at No.4 for many years, and died there in 1941. He was father to the artist C R W Nevinson. No.27 Lawn Road was the home in recent years of Eva Collet Reckitt (1890-1976) of the Reckitt's Blue family: she founded Collet's, the celebrated left-wing bookshop in Charing Cross Road. John Logie Baird (1888-1946), the television pioneer, lived at No.84 in the 1930s. The main architectural interest of Lawn Road is the Grade I-Listed **Isokon** block of flats at the north end of the road.

No.30 Upper Park Road was the home of Stella Gibbons (1902-89), author of *Cold Comfort Farm*. As Park Road, Parkhill Road was the first development on the estate and

still contains many of its original semi-detached, four-storey houses. The sculptor Henry Moore (1898-1986) and his wife Irina lived from 1929 to 1940 at No.11A, where he developed his distinctive abstract style. The Dutch painter Piet Mondrian (1872-1944) lived at No.60 from 1938 until it was bombed in 1940.

St John's Wood

South-west Hampstead was part of a large estate owned by the Knights Hospitaller from 1312. After the Dissolution, the 500 acres in this area became known as St John's Wood and in 1594 was leased by Queen Elizabeth I to Sir William Waad of Belsize, with which for the next 150 years it was closely associated. In 1732 the Earl of Chesterfield, in need of cash, sold St John's Wood to Henry Samuel Eyre (d. 1754), a London wine merchant.

The greater part of the Eyre estate lay in Marylebone, south of what became Boundary Road, which since 1900 has marked the southern limit of Hampstead. It was low-lying and not easily accessible, but the Eyre family was anxious to promote building and in 1794 an unexecuted plan was drawn up on the model of Bath. In the next decade development on the Eyre estate was directed by the young architect John Shaw and began on the Marylebone portion, stimulated further by proximity to Regent's Park.

The area lying within Hampstead was not developed until after **Finchley Road** and **Avenue Road** were laid out in the 1820s. Building activity occurred in the late 1840s and during the 1850s, with large detached houses built in small groups by a number of builders. A school for the blind was built in 1848 at the southern junction of College Crescent and Avenue Road and several times enlarged. Immediately south of the blind school a large house called Sunnyside was built; it was later St Columba's hospital. Enclosed by the curve of College Crescent, the New College of Independent Dissenters, to train ministers, was opened in 1851 in a Tudor-style building.

In 1851 the estate, like Chalcots and Belsize, housed mainly the professional and commercial classes, almost all with several servants. Thereafter the character of new housing, to serve a slightly lower social level, began to change, with westward expansion along roads parallel with the railway and at the western end around Abbey Road and its side-roads. By 1862 most of the area between Avenue Road and Bridge Road was built up with detached and semi-detached houses.

West of Bridge (Loudoun) Road the land sloped to a shallow trough before rising again beyond the Eyre estate. The slope, together with the narrowness of the remaining sites imposed by the railway and estate boundary, contributed to higher-density, mostly terraced housing. Eventually there were 57 stables there, for omnibus horses, and Britannia Terrace, in Belsize Road, and Victoria (Fairfax) Road were built during the later 1850s and early 1860s for the stable staff and drivers and conductors. With transport assured, close-packed middle-class housing followed in the centre, e.g. in Alexandra Road (built after the marriage of the Prince of Wales

in 1863) and Belsize Road to the north. By 1866 building was virtually complete.

By the end of the 1880s, the mews in the south-west, were no longer service areas on the edge of the housing, which had moved beyond them, but pockets classified as 'fairly comfortable, good ordinary earnings'. They declined in status by 1930 when one mews, by then called Fairfax Place, was singled out as one of the worst parts of the borough for overcrowding.

Rebuilding of the area started in the 1930s, when large houses started to give way to blocks of flats, for example around **Avenue Road**, and continued apace after the war, mostly for local authority housing. The whole area around Finchley Road and Avenue Road was transformed by flats. In the 1960s the **Swiss Cottage Centre** was opened and the council in conjunction with the LCC, rebuilt the entire western portion of the estate, west of Abbey Road, from which the new development took its name; high-rise blocks obliterated the street pattern of the old service area. Two large developments in the 1970s transformed the central part of the district, with a long curving swathe of concrete terraces, designed to the highest permissible density by Neave Brown on the site of Alexandra Road. The GLC built the Ainsworth estate east of Abbey Road, north of Boundary Road, mostly by 1970.

Some of the mid-19th century houses have managed to survive this onslaught. A few remain in Boundary Road, including No.7 home for over two decades of the MP, writer and *bon viveur* Sir Clement Freud (1924-2009). Other

survivals are mainly on the better-built eastern side of the estate, including most of the north side of Belsize Road.

St Mary's Holly Place

After the French Revolution there was a small but noticeable influx of émigrés into Hampstead, including Abbé Morel who came to the town from Sussex in 1796 and from the first acted as pastor to its Catholics. To make ends meet he taught his native tongue. The congregation met for many years at Oriel House in now demolished Little Church Row. In 1816 Morel had raised enough money to complete St Mary's Catholic church, said to be the second oldest Catholic church in London and certainly one of the smallest. A simple building, light and colourful inside with mosaics behind the altar, its front is conspicuously decorated with a handsome statue of the Virgin and Child in a niche. A later exile from France, who also worshipped here, was Charles de Gaulle. Judi Dench and Michael Williams were married here in 1971.

St Stephen's

This weighty church was built in 1869 on **Hampstead Green**, on a site given by Sir Thomas Maryon Wilson and funded by public subscription. It was designed in a Gothic style by the architect S S Teulon. Some consider it his best work. Teulon used purple-red Dunstable brick, with bands of ragstone and granite. Ruskin hailed it as "the finest specimen of brick-building in all the land", although others were not so favourable: "half a

St Mary's, Holly Place, c. 1912.

St Stephen's, at Hampstead Green, early 20th century.

House of God, half a castle on the Rhine". It cost three times the original estimate, with rich ornament inside and out; some of the glass was by Clayton & Bell.

St Stephen's was built to seat 1,250, but its steeply sloping site meant it was always prone to subsidence. Very worrying cracks appeared when the foundations of the new Royal Free Hospital were escavated. A few years later, in 1977, high maintenance costs and a declining congregation forced the closure of the church. For twenty years it stood empty and vandals and squatters despoiled the building, while arguments about its future use raged. Then in 1999 the St Stephen's Restoration and Preservation Trust was awarded the lease, to restore the building to life as a community resource. Well over £4 million was raised from the Heritage Lottery Fund, English Heritage, local businesses and individual donors through the efforts of the adjoining Hampstead Nursery School (led by architect Michael Taylor). The building reopened in 2009.

St Stephen's built a mission hall in Denning Road. Long known as Denning Hall, the building is still inscribed "Asked of God, 1883", although since then it has had a wide variety of uses.

The Salvation Army

The Army registered the Athenaeum hall in the **Vale of Health** in 1882. It led processions from here across the Heath but stopped these because its members were mimicked and attacked by ruffians. Lacking financial support it gave up the hall in 1886, when the bonfire on the adjoining Heath burned an effigy not of Guy Fawkes but of a Salvation Army commandant. The Army then opened a mission room in New Buildings, **Flask Walk**. A new Salvation Army barracks and hall, was built in Flask Walk in 1905 and lasted until 1971.

Schools

The earliest school in Hampstead was in a tree. In the 1650s there was said to be a school for twelve young gentlemen in the **Hollow Tree**, which **Barratt** with rare humour wrote "gave Hampstead a start in Higher Education"! In 1684 there was a school at New End, run by Lancelott Johnson.

Emmanuel School in Mill Lane, West Hampstead – the building, designed by Charles Miles, son of the owners of West End House, still stands. Emmanuel is a Voluntary Aided Church of England school.

The large houses of Hampstead were eminently suitable for private schools. On the 1851 census 39 private day schools are recorded and by 1872 60 were listed. In that year Heath Mount School at the top of Heath Street prepared day boys and boarders for the Civil Service, the armed services, and public schools. It was variously said to have been founded in 1795 and 1817. Evelyn Waugh, Cecil Beaton and Gerald **du Maurier** attended. The school had closed here by 1934.

Nos.1&2 Mortimer Crescent, Kilburn formed the private Henley House school, bought in 1878 by John Vine Milne, father of A A Milne who lived and was taught here; a young H G Wells (1866-1946) was the school's first science teacher in 1889. Alfred Harmsworth (1865-1922) was encouraged to start the school magazine in 1878, printed from 1881. By 1893 Milne had moved his school to Westgate-on-Sea; Henley House continued as a school until about 1910 under a succession of proprietors.

Hall School moved into its building in Crossfield Road in 1905. This had originally been a girls' school founded in 1890 by the Misses Allen-Olney; their initials are in the brickwork beside the front door. In 1989 Hall School celebrated its centenary by publishing its history and building an extension followed by another across the road in 1997. Old Boys of The Hall, known as Old Aularians, include Clement Freud, John Schlesinger and Peter Shaffer.

University College School which opened in Frognal in 1907 has the biggest presence today. The most famous private school for girls is probably the **South Hampstead High School**, but before World War Two, No.104 Fitzjohn's Avenue was the prestigious Frognal School for Girls. In the 1920s, its ex-Roedean headmistresses were offering education 'on public school lines', including Swedish drill twice weekly. The school song was *Frognal, Frognal, high on the hill.*

Free education in Hamp-

stead was first provided by the church. The **Hampstead Parochial School** was begun in 1790. Emmanuel School in West Hampstead when it opened in 1846 consisted of one classroom and a cottage for its mistress, built on a small piece of ground given by the owner of neighbouring Cholmley Lodge (eventually demolished in 1914). At the time it was Hampstead's smallest church school launched so that the children of West End would not miss their "pious exercises and the godly discipline of labour" because of the uphill trudge to the church. The buildings were enlarged in 1872 and again twenty years later. Church schools were known as National schools while schools run by Nonconformists were called British Schools, the first in Hampstead opened in 1862 in Heath Street, next to the new Baptist chapel.

After 1870 the state began to provide education. The first board school in Hampstead was the Fleet Primary, in Fleet Road, which opened in 1879. By the 1890s under the inspired leadership of Henry Adams and his wife it became known as the 'Harrow of the board schools', regularly winning scholarships to secondary schools. Its reputation meant that by 1900 it was no longer taking only local poor but drawing children from a considerable distance. By then the London School Board had also founded large schools at the foot of Haverstock Hill and in Netherwood Street, Kilburn. In 1905-06 the dramatically tall New End School was built with some ingenuity over a source of the River Fleet, squeezed onto a tiny hillside site.

Among present compre-

The Sailors' Daughters' Home in Fitzjohn's Avenue in 1869. It has since been converted to old-people's flats.

hensive schools one to note is Hampstead School in Westbere Road near the borough boundary. In 1961 this large school took over and added to buildings used by Haberdashers' Aske's School based here between 1898 and 1961, following its move from Hoxton where it had been set up by the will of Robert Aske (d.1689) as a school for twenty sons of poor freemen of the Company. The coat of arms of the Haberdashers' Company remains with its injunction to 'Serve and Obey'.

Other educational establishments have included the Royal Sailors' Orphan Girls' School and Home opened in Hampstead in 1862 at Frognal House, with asylum for 100 girls, and education as domestic servants. In 1869 it moved to a new building at Nos.96-116 Fitzjohn's Avenue, designed by Edward Ellis. The Home closed in 1957 and was converted to old people's flats, named after the home's long-serving secretary, F R D'O Monro, also secretary to the **Wells Trust**. No.339 Finchley Road began as the International College in 1885, designed in free Gothic style by the architect, Banister Fletcher. The original building had a tower containing an astronomical observatory, dormitories for some 100 boarders and a hall to seat 800 scholars. The college's promoter and principal was James Haysman, who had already opened the Anglo-French College in what is now Burgess Hill to the north in 1873: both institutions were run on his System of International Education, which stressed the value of learning modern languages, science and art. The college left Finchley Road in 1907 and the building was divided into smaller units.

Sewers

Before the main drainage system was constructed from 1859 onwards, Hampstead relied largely on cesspools which drained into the soil, contaminating water supplies, or into streams and ditches suitable only for surface water. As the town was near the top of a hill, up until the 1840s drainage was not seen as a problem. Then cholera heightened awareness and complaints began to be made about crowded alleys and courts. Under the Metropolis Local Management Act, 1855, the Vestry could raise money for building sewers and by 1872 the whole parish drained into the Metropolitan Board of Works' system, the eastern part into the high-level 'intercepting' sewer that ran from Hampstead to Stratford, taking in the waters of the Fleet; and the Kilburn area into the Ranelagh sewer. Of more than 22 miles, just over half were constructed by the Vestry, the rest at private expense.

Shepherd's Well

This was once a major source of Hampstead's **water supply**, now marked by a plaque at the forked junction of Akenside and Lyndhurst Roads with Fitzjohn's Avenue. The well disappeared when the Avenue was built in the 1870s. It was the headwater of the River Tyburn, which flows (now in conduits) to the Thames via the lake in Regent's Park and past Buckingham Palace.

It had the purest of waters, which never froze in the hardest of winters. In the summer water carriers, who charged one penny per bucket, sometimes had to queue at the well for hours. It has been recorded that the last of these old water-carriers died an inmate of the workhouse at New End about 1868.

By 1801 a conduit led from the well to a cistern at the bottom of the Grove, Rosslyn Hill, opposite Pond Street whose inhabitants were supplied from it. With the coming of the New River Company's piped **water**

Shepherd's Well at the junction of today's Akenside and Lyndhurst roads.

supply the spring lost favour and, when the local land went up for sale, was described as "filthy and disreputable". It was reconstructed as a drinking fountain, and remodelled again in 1936, but vandalism led to the fountain's removal in the 1980s.

Shoot-up Hill

This is part of the Roman Watling Street leading from Dover to Chester. Although first shown on Rocque's map of 1746 the name Shoot-up Hill was not officially approved until 1899. Its derivation is unknown, but many claim it comes from Henry VIII shooting game in the Forest of Middlesex. It is now lined by several blocks of flats, including Hillcrest Court, home in the late 1930s to the young sisters Jackie and Joan Collins and the large Templar House, completed in 1954.

The latter recalls the Knights Templar, owners in 1312 of the Temple estate, to the east of the road, which had been parcelled out of manorial lands held by the abbots of Westminster. In that year the Pope broke up the Knights Templar order and transferred its possessions to the Knights Hospitallers of St John of Jerusalem. At the Dissolution the estate was given to Sir Roger Cholmeley (c.1485-1565), founder of Highgate School. There is unlikely to have been a dwelling house on the Temple estate earlier than the one which the prior of the Hospitallers was said in 1522 to have made at his own expense, probably on the site of the later Shoot Up Hill Farm,

which certainly existed by the 1580s, on the Edgware Road just south of its junction with Shoot Up Hill Lane.

The freehold of Shoot Up Hill Farm was bought in 1773 by John Powell of Fulham and inherited in 1838 by Captain Henry Cotton, after which the property was part of the so-called Powell-Cotton estate. The family owned land in the Thanet area of Kent, including Quex Park – hence the Kentish names of most of the roads in this area, developed from the 1870s. Fordwych Road, from Mill Lane to Maygrove Road, defined the estate's eastern boundary. At its northern end shops and dwellings were built in the Parade, Cricklewood, and in Richborough Road in the 1890s. Some of the farm buildings, which by then surrounded an imposing residence called Kingsgate Lodge, survived until the start of the 20th century, after which Kingscroft Road was laid across the site in 1912-13. Fanny Brawne (1800-65), the fiancée of John Keats, had lived as a child in a neighbouring farm, called Royston Hall.

The six-million gallon Shoot-up Hill reservoir,

Shoot-up Hill c.1905.

originally developed by the Grand Junction Company, is now encircled by Gondar Gardens. This and neighbouring streets, fully developed in the Edwardian period, were named after places in East Africa frequented by intrepid big-game hunter Major Percy Powell-Cotton.

Leading off Shoot-up Hill, Mill Lane was once known as Shoot Up Hill Lane or alternatively Windmill Lane, after a windmill burnt down in 1861 following a gale that blew the sails round so ferociously that they caught fire.

Above is W H Smith in Swiss Terrace, Finchley Road, then also a circulating library. Below is Cresswell's in Kingsgate Road, one of the many small dairies which delivered milk by cart.

Shops

The High Street was the first main shopping area of Hampstead. Over the years many of its small and useful shops that served the community have gone, e.g. Gaze's haberdashers, which traded at Nos.65&66. Until 1979 Fowler's at No.40 had been in the same line of business since the 1850s when the proprietor was an oil and colourman, whose trade signs were the oil jars attached to the façade (now in **Hampstead Museum**). For decades No.29 was Stamp the chemist. The flat above is supposedly haunted; here the actor Leo McKern (1920-2002) led séances in the 1970s.

As in many High Streets there are increasing numbers of estate agents, but here there are also swish shops for the affluent and it is dense with delicatessens. Neighbouring Heath Street also has a fair number of shops. Its southern end was built up in the late 1880s with red-brick shopping parades, mainly by E J Cave. Businesses are varied and include the Louis Patisserie,

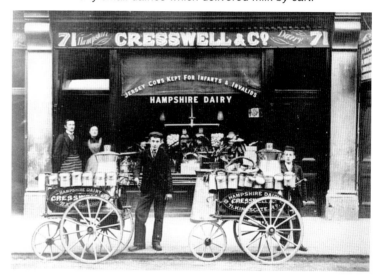

founded by Hungarian refugees in the 1950s – a slice of old Vienna.

The largest and liveliest shopping street in Hampstead has always been Kilburn High Road. The growth of West Hampstead changed its face in the late Victorian period. By 1900 small shops were disappearing to be replaced by larger emporia. Alongside grandiose buildings for banks and entertainment, several chain stores opened branches. By 1909 there were over 300

shops, including over 40 drapery and allied trades. Marks & Spencer which opened at Nos.66-68 about 1930, had started with a Penny Bazaar on the other side of the High Road in 1907. The High Road's most famous department store was B B Evans. Benjamin Beardmore Evans started here as a draper in a single terraced house in 1897. Neighbouring houses were soon acquired and remodelled, with more rebuilding after a serious fire in 1910. B B Evans

The B B Evans store in Kilburn High Road ablaze in 1910.

was sold to Canadian & English Stores in 1962, when it employed more than 500 people. It was Kilburn's only department store by the time of its closure in 1971, when it was divided up between shops at Nos.142-162. Today the street still has its chain stores, a fair

Mrs Emerson's butcher's shop at 51 Heath Street, 1903.

sprinkling of discount outlets and a very cosmopolitan feel.

Finchley Road never fulfilled its promise as a shopping street and its very heavy traffic does not make it a pleasant place to browse. It did however have the largest department store in the borough: John Barnes & Co. The company, which started trading in 1900, was described as 'American style' in that it did not expand from small beginnings but was financed by a syndicate, including directors of Dickins & Jones of Regent Street. The intention was to profit from the spread of building around Fitzjohn's Avenue by providing a lavishly appointed store, with 37 departments and a workforce of nearly 400. John Barnes was taken over by Selfridge's in 1926. In 1936 the mayor declared that the store's rebuilding would make Finchley Road "the Regent

Street of north London". The new building in the popular ocean-liner style of the period held the stores on three floors, with five floors of flats, called St. John's Court, overhead. The John Lewis Partnership, however, which acquired John Barnes in 1940, found the site too cramped and tried vainly to sell it in the 1960s. John Barnes closed in 1981 and part of the Finchley Road building now houses a Waitrose supermarket. A recent addition to Finchley Road has been the O_2 shopping centre, housing a multiplex cinema, various eateries and shops, including a large Waterstone's bookstore.

Slums

Not a word that springs to mind with Hampstead but the area always had its fair share of poor inhabitants. In 1653 Hampstead pleaded poverty on the grounds that 'divers

Church Place, one of the slum alleyways in the network around the parish church before Fitzjohn's Avenue was extended to Heath Street.

Perrin's Court survived the rebuilding of the upper part of the High Street and the extension of Fitzjohn's Avenue to Heath Street. Watercolour by Mary Hill in the 1930s.

houses' were occupied by citizens who paid their taxes in London and many inhabitants were poor wage-earning labourers at the tile kilns, while their wives washed clothes for Londoners. The low-lying New End long remained a poor area.

But poverty in itself does not produce slums. These developed to the west of the High Street where in a jumble of courtyards and alleys between Perrin's Lane and Holly Hill the tenements were old, ill-built but most importantly overcrowded. By the mid 19th century many families were living in single rooms because rents were high. There were several lodging houses and residences became multiple dwellings. Thorne, in his *Environs of London* refers to "narrow and dirty byways, courts, and passages, with steep flights of steps, and mean and crowded tenements" which led off the High Street.

Little Church Row was a dilapidated alleyway off which were several decaying courtyards. The largest was

Yorkshire Grey Yard surrounding the Yorkshire Grey inn, used sometimes for inquests. Some of the worst slums were in Bradley's Buildings (on the site of the **Everyman**) and Crockett's Court. Dr Charles Lord, Hampstead's first Medical Officer of Health from 1856-79, in his book of personal reminiscences, noted that the most dirty, ill-ventilated and overcrowded houses were in Crockett's Court. This was pulled down in 1877 and Wells

Buildings erected over it.

The development of the high-class Fitzjohn's Avenue to the south highlighted the conditions at the top of the hill and the Vestry decided that the slums behind the High Street should be swept away. Traders were not keen as they were concerned that if the Avenue were extended to meet Heath Street, traffic might go straight through the town without passing their shops. But the Hampstead Town Improvements were authorised by the

Metropolitan Street Improvements Act passed in 1883, and the new roads were opened to the public in February 1888. The costs were shared by the Hampstead Vestry and the Board of Works. Oriel Place, shops, and tenement blocks were laid out over the site of the slums.

It was claimed that most of the slum dwellers were rehoused in Campden Buildings, erected in 1886 in Holly Bush Vale and in Wells Buildings – which Booth in 1898 said was full of "good working-class" – but the clearances in the old town led many of the poor to move to West Hampstead and Kilburn, where rents were lower. Other immigrants, from poor parts of London and from Ireland, were competing for rooms there in houses which, though small, were beginning to be divided. Thus developed a cleavage between the wealthy east and the increasingly poor and crowded western parts of Hampstead.

Slyes

A copyhold estate on the west of High Street which probably took its name from the 14th-century Sleigh (Slegh) family. In 1312 it was described as 13½ acres and a house, that traditionally was in the centre of the estate. Sir Harry Vane may have lived here. In 1674 it had 23 hearths and was occupied by Mrs Honywood, presumably Rebecca, wife of Isaac Honywood, possibly while the main Honywood residence, later called Carlile House (*ill. p. 91*), was being built. Between 1712 and 1721 the house was "new built and expanded and converted to four tenements", but in 1762

was again a single house, occupied by the owner Robert Cary. It can probably be identified with The Rookery which was occupied by the publisher Thomas Norton Longman (d.1842) and was demolished in 1870, to be replaced in turn by a Wesleyan chapel and in the 1930s by the Greenhill flats.

Social Clubs

The rich inhabitants of Hampstead town set up several social clubs. The oldest was the **Hampstead Dinner Club**, but others included the Hampstead Conversazione Society, which met monthly during the winter at the Assembly Rooms from 1846 until 1872. In addition to lectures, it provided art exhibitions which for limited periods were open free to all residents.

The Athenaeum club, which, despite its name, was social rather than literary, in 1877 occupied a hotel which had been built near the **Vale of Health** tavern. The owner claimed in 1880 that 1,200 'members' had been added during the past year. His establishment presumably continued as the Anglo-German club, with 500 English and 700 German members in 1908, until the outbreak of World War One in 1914.

Societies

Hampstead has over the years generated an amazing variety of societies. To pick out a few, Hampstead Parliamentary Debating Society was founded in 1883 and met weekly during the winter at the Vestry Hall until 1888, with 500 or more members. In 1891 it became the

Hampstead Parliament, which reproduced the procedure of the House of Commons. It met at the Blind School, Swiss Cottage from 1910, and as 'the oldest local parliament in the kingdom', at the Town Hall in about 1953, shortly before its dissolution.

The Hampstead Conservatoire of Music and School of Art (*see* **Central School of Speech and Drama**) was founded in 1885. Four years later the Hampstead Medical Society was set up at what was called the Hampstead Home Hospital (later Hampstead General). It was formed to discuss subjects of social, scientific and professional interest.

Hampstead Antiquarian and Historical Society was founded in 1897 and first met, at the Vestry hall, in 1898. Sir Walter Besant was president and the local historians Thomas **Barratt** and G W Potter were members. Publication of learned articles in the Society's *Transactions* and more literary ones in its *Hampstead Annual* quickly made Hampstead appear superior to other suburbs in the richness of its historical associations. The Society operated until the Second World War; its descendant is the **Camden History Society**.

In 1925 it was claimed that no other part of London was so intensely organized as Hampstead for intellectual and social clubs, but the number mushroomed by the 1950s when many societies formed a federation called Music and Arts in Hampstead, through which they received municipal sponsorship.

The pond at South End Green, now the site of a bus turn-around. Parliament Hill is in the background.

South End Green

South End Green was created in 1835 when the pond which had given Pond Street its name was filled in, although the name does not appear on a map until 1847. The isolated village at the eastern end of Pond Street was affected by the crowds of trippers at Hampstead Heath station after 1860, and by building at South Hill Park and the laying out of the Fleet and Constantine Roads in the 1870s and 1880s. But it was transformed by the London Street Tramways Company's extension to a terminus there in 1887 which cut a swathe through the green. At the time of Bank Holiday fairs, trams would arrive at the rate of one a minute. From 1887 the old houses and cottages were replaced by red-brick shops and flats, including

Maryon Terrace. It soon became a major traffic centre, which it has remained.

In 1910 a local commentator noted that the only green left in South End Green was the paint on the railings round the fountain. This public fountain, now protected by the South End Green Association, was presented in 1880 by Miss Anne Crump "to help stop intemperance and vice". She lived in Hereford House on the south side of the Green, a house pulled down in 1913 and replaced by the Hampstead Picture Playhouse, which became the Classic and then Cannon cinema – and finally the ABC, which closed in 2000. A Marks & Spencer food store now covers the site.

The public lavatories across the road were built in 1897 for

The renovated fountain at South End Green, 2009.

South Hampstead High School for Girls c.1905.

South Hill Park

The arrival of the railway in 1860 cut off the South Hill Park area from the rest of the Belsize estate, of which it was once a part. The three remaining fields to the north were developed from the 1870s, partly by Thomas Rhodes of St Pancras, whose family since 1804 had held the old copyhold estate called Duddingtons in this area, and partly by the farmer Joseph Pickett. The new streets were laid out to maximise frontages but the houses turned their backs to the Heath. Aimed at the respectable middle-class the development had to contend with proximity to the tramway which opened in 1887 and the distinctly lower-class area of Fleet Road. The turning called Park End was to become a hive of small industries.

In South Hill Park itself the first building was the **Magdala** pub, erected in 1868. No.57 was briefly the home of Andrew Fisher (1862-1928), who rose from pitboy to be thrice Prime Minister of Australia: he died here in 1928. No.93 near the top of the hill, was the home of guitarist John Williams in the

use by passengers at the tram terminus. They have delicate wrought-iron work and were Listed in 1993, one of the few remaining Victorian lavatories in London. A scene in *Prick Up Your Ears*, the 1987 film about Joe Orton, was shot here.

South Hampstead High School for Girls

This selective, academic day school for girls began life in 1876 as the St John's Wood High School in Winchester Road, Swiss Cottage. It became South Hampstead High School for Girls when it moved to Maresfield Gardens. The new school was opened in 1882 by Princess Louise in a building designed by E C Robins. Since the war, the school has acquired several adjoining sites, including the home of Sir Ernest Waterlow RA, which the school demolished but commemorated in its Waterlow

building of 1988. The Junior Department is housed in two Victorian mansions in nearby Netherhall Gardens and the sixth form has its own building, Oakwood House. Alumni include actresses Angela Lansbury and Helena Bonham-Carter, and the writer Fay Weldon.

South Hill Park.

The Spaniard's Inn at the beginning of the 20th century before the distance between it and the surviving tollhouse became a traffic stopper. They stand where Hampstead Lane and Spaniard's Road meet.

1970s. The writer and director Anthony Minghella (b. 1954) died at No.26 in 2008.

The road called Parliament Hill is named after the nearby eminence on Hampstead Heath. Joseph Pickett began building here over his old farmland in 1880. Some of the first houses were built for the Hampstead Home Hospital, which rapidly expanded into South Hill Park and in 1904 metamorphosed into the Hampstead General Hospital bordering Hampstead Green. No.68 was the final home of the poet Anna Wickham (1883-1947) who was famous for her artistic salons, which included D H Lawrence, Edith Sitwell and many impecunious writers, such as Dylan Thomas. There is a plaque to George Orwell (1903-50) on No.77, where the writer lodged for barely six months in 1935.

Spaniard's Inn

This is probably the most celebrated of Hampstead's pubs, although it is technically in the Borough of Barnet, as the boundary stones show. The present pub is an early-18th-century building with low ceilings and a number of tiny parlours in addition to the main bar, hung with prints, muskets, pistols and other atmospheric items.

Tradition has it that Spain's ambassador to the court of James I had a house on this site, and that his valet later started an inn. More likely, the name derives from the Spanish licensee registered in 1721.

Here was also the lodge house and toll-gate for the Bishop of London's park, which stretched to the top of Highgate Hill (site of another toll-gate); the colony was then

known as Parkgate. The 18th-century toll-house, which narrows the road at a sharp corner and still slows down the traffic, was rescued by the **Heath and Hampstead Society** in 1967 and repaired.

In the 18th century Hampstead Wells brought rich custom for the tavern and its pleasure gardens, which Park records were "improved and beautifully ornamented" by a Mr. William Staples, who, "out of a wild and thorny wood … hath now made pleasant grass and gravel walks, with a mount, from the elevation whereof the beholder hath a prospect of Hanslope steeple, in North-amptonshire". This seems rather unlikely, but the prospect was altered by the erection of two or three large houses nearby. The grounds had a bowling green, an artificial mound and mechanical tableaux, depicted by Chatelaine in 1750.

In the Gordon Riots of 1780, nearby Kenwood House, then occupied by the Earl of Mansfield (1705-93), was saved from destruction — unlike his town house — when the landlord of the Spaniard's offered the rioters unlimited refreshment at the inn. This delayed them sufficiently until the military, already alerted by the Mansfield family, arrived.

The inn was popular with Dickens (1812-70), who placed the arrest of Mrs Bardell in *The Pickwick Papers* here.

Spaniard's Quarter

This is the convenient 18th-century name for the group of houses that were built close to the Spaniard's Inn. Heath End House was the first, put up in 1734 by John Turner, a rich merchant, who is credited with building the sandy road that still runs from here to North End. He also planted a clump of firs, which were frequently recorded by artists, including **Constable**. All the desirable 18th-century cottages in Spaniards End, which descends into Barnet, were converted from the stables and garden sheds of this house whose name was changed to the Firs. It was converted into two houses in the 1950s and the billiard room became Casa Maria, in a Spanish style.

Present-day Evergreen Hill was once part of Heath End House. It was the home of the Arctic explorer, Sir William Parry (1790-1855); and from 1889 to 1912 of Canon Samuel Barnett (1844-1913) and his wife, otherwise Dame Henrietta Barnett (1851-1936), prime promoter of Hampstead Garden Suburb. In 1895 they

lent their home to the American painter Whistler, whose wife died here, and in 1903 they took over Erskine House for a convalescent home.

Erskine House itself was demolished in 1923 and the present building is adapted from one of its wings. The original 18th-century house was the home in the 1760s of John Sanderson, architect of the parish church, and from 1788 of the advocate Thomas Lord Erskine (1750-1823). A forensic genius, who even won the acquittal of the riotous Lord Gordon, and Lord Chancellor in 1806-07, he lived here until 1821. He expanded his garden across the road by building a tunnel and planted so many bays and laurels that he called his property Evergreen Hill.

On the opposite side of Spaniards Road stands The Elms, a mansion built in about 1875 on the site of Mother Huff's Tea Gardens, which flourished here for 50 years (or so Mother Huff claimed) in 1728). Mother Huff's was cited in Baker's comedy *Hampstead Heath*, performed at Drury Lane in 1705. The Elms was home from 1894 to 1908 to the art dealer Sir Joseph Joel Duveen (1869-1939), who added the Duveen Gallery to the British Museum and the Turner Wing to the Tate Gallery. From 1957 it housed St Columba's hospital and was then owned, but rarely inhabited, by Barbara Hutton (1912-79), the Wool-worth heiress. In 1981 it was sold for a large sum to the president of the United Arab Emirates but it remained unoccupied and in 1987 was sold to developers.

Squire's Mount

The house took its name from Joshua Squire (d.1717), a London factor who built a terrace of four houses in 1714 on waste he had acquired. The terrace was later converted into two: Chestnut Lodge and the main Squire's Mount. The family of Edwin Field (1804-71), the law reformer, lived in this house for many years and were to leave it to the National Trust. In the 1930s it was occupied by the film star Clive Brook.

Squire's Mount is also the name of the adjoining short road. A terrace of pretty cottages, Nos.1-5, bears a plate 'Squires Mount Croft 1704', but they did not exist in 1762 so the plate may have come from the stabling of Squire's Mount. Nos.11&12 look older but were only built in the 1950s. Actor Richard Burton was an early inhabitant, soon joined by Elizabeth Taylor and family. Composer Sandy Wilson lived at No.12.

Stanfield House

Now divided into Nos.85-89 Hampstead High Street, Stanfield House (*see illustration on p.83*) was built about 1730 as part of a terrace of three and commemorates the artist Clarkson Stanfield (1793-1867). He lived here from 1847 to 1876 and was visited by his friend Dickens. He was driven away by the development of Prince Arthur Road, which demo-lished two-thirds of the terrace, and died in Belsize Park Gardens. The house became a hospital, then a school until, in 1885, the Hampstead Sub-scription Library moved in to remain for over eighty years. Subsequently housing a

Squire's Mount cottages 1911. Drawing by A R Quinton.

Christian Science church from 1966, it is now private residences.

Steele's Cottage

A cottage on **Haverstock Hill**, opposite the **Load of Hay**, which had been the last home of the politician and writer Charles Sedley (c.1639-1701), who died here in poverty; his daughter Catherine was the wealthy mistress of James II who made her Countess of Dorchester. From 1713 the cottage was taken by the writer Sir Richard Steele (c.1672-1729). It was near enough to Hampstead to enable him to attend the meetings of the Kit Cat Club at the Upper Flask and far enough from the City and his creditors there. Steele's Cottage and its fine view over London and St Paul's appeared in many prints and paintings, notably in one by Constable in 1832. It was pulled down in 1867 to make way for a row of shops and Steele's Road. The writer is also remembered in the area by the nearby Victorian gin palace, The Sir Richard Steele.

Swiss Cottage

A new tavern at the start of Finchley Road, and at the junction with six other roads, is first mentioned in the Rate Books of 1840. It stood next to the toll gate and was built to resemble a Swiss chalet, then all the rage. Although much rebuilt and extended, (Ye Olde) Swiss Cottage Tavern still displays this style.

The Swiss Cottage gave its name to the surrounding area on the **St John's Wood** estate, which acquired a bus terminus

Steele's Cottage on Haverstock Hill on the right, with the Load of Hay opposite and London in the distance. Painting by John Constable c. 1832.

An early Swiss Cottage tavern c.1905. Two horse buses are at rest, advertising the fact that they go over Westminster Bridge.

in 1856 and a station on the Underground (then the Metropolitan Railway) in 1868.

Until 1873 travellers might pause at the pub before paying their fees to use Finchley Road at the Junction Road Toll Gate. Baines wrote in 1890 that the Swiss Cottage was a noted meeting place for 'running men' who ran races in Finchley Road.

The rest of the central island here was altered in the late 1930s, when the Odeon cinema was erected. The Swiss Cottage area was massively redeveloped after the war, notably for the construction of the **Swiss Cottage Centre**.

Swiss Cottage Centre

The area to the east of Avenue Road was cleared by Hampstead Borough Council in the 1950s to be developed into a new Civic Centre. Basil Spence (1907-76) published a scheme for this in 1959 and parts of it, the Library and Sports Centre, were opened in 1964 by the Queen. Further plans were complicated by the formation of Camden borough in 1965, for this entailed the scrapping of the old schemes when the new borough's administration was centred on Euston Road instead. After much discussion, part of the Swiss Cottage site was sold to London and Paris Holdings in 1981, resulting in an office block at the north-west corner, and an open space known by some as Swiss Cottage Green.

From the late 1990s Camden Council announced plans to

The new Swiss Cottage Centre, with the Leisure Centre to the left and Basil Spence's library to the right.

regenerate the Swiss Cottage Centre. The Library had a make-over in 2002-03 with more light and accessibility, a colourful Children's Library and the Swiss Cottage Art Gallery. Opposite the Library entrance is a bronze abstract sculpture by Frederick McWilliam (1964) called the *Hampstead Figure*. The Council's plans were completed by 2007 at a cost of some £85m, after the Sports Centre was demolished and replaced by a glass Leisure Centre. This was designed by Sir Terry Farrell (b. 1939), with two swimming pools and many other sporting facilities, such as a climbing wall on the Adelaide Road frontage. The complex includes affordable flats, a community centre and a doctor's surgery. Alongside is a block of luxury apartments called The Visage. The 'green' has become Swiss Cottage Park.

Hampstead Town Hall c. 1905, described by Pevsner as 'crushingly mean'.

Theatres

As early as 1709 a playhouse had been erected, but it closed down shortly afterwards due to local opposition. The Manor Court in July that year directed its constables "to apprehend the players that they may be punished as rogues, vaga-bonds, and sturdy beggars". A century later, 'Gyngell's theatre of mirth and mechanism' appeared in a booth at Hampstead Square in 1805 and a new theatre was advertised in 1817 at the **Assembly Rooms**, although no permanent theatre was established.

It was not until the late 19th century that Hampstead became a centre of theatrical activity, with the town becoming home to actors, such as Beerbohm Tree and a

number of theatres opening. The Theatre Royal, Kilburn, was opened in 1886 and altered in 1895, to hold just over 500. It was known by 1903 as the Kilburn Empire Theatre of Varieties, No.256 Belsize Road, and was still a theatre of varieties in 1910, when it was also being used as a cinema, later called the Kilburn Palace. Nearby the New Empire Theatre of Varieties was built in 1907, which became the **Kilburn Empire**. Kilburn was so popular as a place of entertainment that on the sale of The Grange in 1910 Sir Oswald Stoll proposed a Coliseum on the lines of his London theatre in St Martin's Lane, but was thwarted by the council.

The theatre tradition has flourished in Hampstead with the **Everyman** which opened in 1920 and the Embassy in 1928 (*see* **Central School of Speech and Drama**). German Jewish refugees started the Little Theatre at No.37A Upper Park Road in 1940 and the

Hampstead Theatre was begun in 1959. The small New End theatre has used the former **mortuary** since 1974.

Town Hall

Hampstead Vestry, later Town, Hall was built in Haverstock Hill in 1877-78 to designs by the district surveyor, H E Kendall. The red-brick and stone Italianate building, with its towering belvedere, was much admired at the time, but was to be derided by Pevsner as "crushingly mean, a disgrace to so prosperous and artistic a borough".

The Town Hall was extended in 1911 to house municipal departments which had grown too large for their offices. By the late 1930s accommodation had again become inadequate but plans were interrupted by the war; thereafter other buildings at Haverstock Hill were also used. A new town hall was projected as part of a Civic Centre at Swiss Cottage but was not required once Camden was formed in 1965.

The building then became the new Borough Engineer's and Borough Surveyor's Department but in 1994 was closed by Camden who considered selling it. However, it became a Listed Building and the **Heath and Hampstead Society** led the community in the campaign to restore it. The refurbished building was opened by the Prince of Wales in June 2000. Users of the revamped Town Hall include various small enterprises and charities, such as the University of the Third Age. A large part of the building is devoted to Interchange Studios, which provides specialist facilities for young people and the disabled.

C. FRANKLIN,
Wine and Spirit Merchant,
BIRD-IN-HAND,
High Street, Hampstead,
(BETWEEN HAMILTON AND WOODWARD'S COACH OFFICES).

Advertisement for the Bird-in-Hand pub just south of Flask Walk, c.1830, advertising its adjacency to two coach offices.

Transport

John Duffield, shortly to become the proprietor of Hampstead Wells, was advertising regular coaches to London as early as 1700. However, stage coaches remained too infrequent for daily business travel until the late 18th century. By 1825 Hampstead was the terminus for ten coaches from the City, when most of them started from the Bird-in-Hand at the top of High Street and ran down Haverstock Hill to Camden Town. The horses were changed, fed and watered in Norway Yard south of Flask Walk.

Coaches provided the only public conveyance to London until the mid 1830s, when Alexander Hamilton started running omnibuses along the same route. In 1856 most of the omnibuses were acquired by the company that became the London General Omnibus Co. (or LGOC). At this time, less than half of Hampstead's c.800

commuters could have been carried by public road transport.

Horse omnibus routes were pushed farther north with the spread of building and opening of suburban **railways**. By 1880 they not only stretched along Kilburn High Road to Brondesbury but also served West Kilburn and West Hampstead by way of Abbey Road and the area north of Swiss Cottage. Services also became more frequent. In 1890 the LGOC's yellow cars left High Street every eighteen minutes.

Horse trams, owned by London Street Tramways, reached Southampton Road on the Hampstead boundary in 1880 and pushed through to South End Green in 1887. A large stables and depot were built near the terminus. A loop was formed by a one-way extension along Agincourt Road. This was the last in London specifically for horse trams; the lines to and from South End were electrified in

1909. Trams were seen as a working-class form of transport and Hampstead traders and carriage-owners successfully opposed them penetrating farther into the parish; proposals for a cable tram up the steep climb of Haverstock Hill were rejected in the 1880s when a similar scheme was introduced in Highgate.

Motorbuses had replaced horse omnibuses by 1911, although Hampstead town and the Heath remained free of public road transport until an east-west service from Finsbury Park to Golders Green via Jack Straw's Castle was started in 1922. Objections by residents prevented any routes through the town until a single-decker service was finally opened in 1968.

The **Hampstead Tube** line, promoted by Charles Yerkes, had opened in 1907 giving easy and speedy access to the West End.

University College School

One of the best independent schools in the country, University College School was first opened in December 1830 in Gower Street as a preparatory school for the new, independent University College, London. It flourished as a day school with no religious education and no corporal punishment (no God and no rod) preparing boys for careers in commerce, but by the end of the Victorian period numbers had fallen. Partly to stem the tide a junior school with about 200 boys was set up in 1891 at 17th-century Holly Hill House (No.11 Holly Hill), rebuilt in 1926-28 to a design by Sir John Simpson.

The senior boys also came to Hampstead when the university needed space and a special Act of Parliament in 1905 separated the school from the College, who provided £60,000 for new buildings. Unfortunately, the site in Frognal was poorly chosen. On the side of a hill, riddled with springs contributing to the River Westbourne, the whole edifice designed by Arnold Mitchell had to be raised over a crypt, and the surrounding grounds were at first a desert on which were dumped excavations from the **Hampstead Tube**.

The opening ceremony on 26 July 1907 was performed by King Edward VII, whose statue appears above the main door. Numbers increased steadily to reach 525 in 1930, and the reputation of the school rose under Cecil Walton from 1936. Finances were secured by realistic fees. Its grounds were beautifully laid out after the

King Edward VII opening the new University College School in Frognal in 1907.

Second World War, when competition for places increased and the school became strong in classics. The main building was damaged by fire in 1978, but the imposing Neo-Georgian pile was rebuilt, its splendid hall restored by Michael Foster, and opened by Queen Elizabeth II in 1980.

Alumni of the school are still referred to as "Old Gowers" in reference to the original site on Gower Street and include Joseph Chamberlain, Walter Sickert, Stephen Spender, William de Morgan, Dirk Bogarde, Roger Bannister and Will Self.

The Upper Flask

This tavern on the east side of the upper end of **Heath Street** was known in 1707 as the Upper Bowling-green House after its very fine green. Its gardens became "a sort of petit Vauxhall" on gala nights, popular with visitors to the spa. It achieved fame as the summer meeting-place of the Kit-Cat Club. This group of cultured and distinguished Whigs, named after pies made by their favourite tavern-keeper Christopher Cat, was a powerful force, both politically and intellectually, in the period up to 1720. Kneller's portraits of its members can be seen at the National Portrait Gallery.

The tavern was later celebrated by Samuel Richardson, in his best-selling novel *Clarissa Harlowe* (1748), in which the persecuted heroine alights there from the Hampstead coach. The tavern closed a few years later and the building became a private residence known as Upper Heath, subsequently the home of George Steevens (1736-1800), the indefatigable annotator of Shakespeare. Upper Heath was replaced by Queen Mary's Maternity Hospital which opened in 1922.

The Upper Flask, drawn by A R Quinton in 1911. By then it was a private house.

Vale of Health

Traditionally, this was supposed to be a place of refuge for Londoners fleeing the Great Plague, but this settlement nestling on the Heath was then no more than a stagnant bog called Gangmoor. Here Samuel Hatch, a harness maker, was granted a piece of waste and built a workshop and then a cottage, hence its 18th-century name of Hatch's Bottom. In 1777 the Hampstead Water Company drained the marshy ground and enlarged the pond into a reservoir. Three cottages were built there for the poor in 1779, to replace those which passed into private ownership at the increasingly fashionable **Littleworth**.

There were tan pits at Hatch's Bottom at the time, replaced by 1808 by a varnish factory. The place was also used for laundering. The name Vale of Health, recorded in 1801, was probably invented in a deliberate attempt to change its image, possibly by the builder of nine dwellings that were sold that year. Middle-

class residents began to be attracted and by 1821 were petitioning for the removal of the poor houses, eventually demolished in the 1850s. Sir Samuel Romilly, the law reformer, retired to a cottage in the Vale and from 1816 **Leigh Hunt** lived here. His home became the centre for most of the leading literary figures of the day.

In the early 1830s the publisher Charles Knight (1791-1873) had his home in the Vale, as did his friend Matthew Davenport Hill (1792-1872), lawyer and radical MP and brother of Rowland. Knight and Hill together established the *Penny Magazine* in 1832 and formed the Society for the Diffusion of Useful Knowledge. Prince Esterhazy was said to have taken a house here in 1840 and the lyricist Lady Dufferin was staying at Pavilion Cottage in the late 1850s, before she moved to Highgate.

The hamlet still had only fourteen houses in 1861. After the Hampstead Junction Railway opened in 1860, it became increasingly desirable and more houses were built. The developer John Culverhouse, who lived at No.5 Villas-on-the-Heath, owned the nearby East Heath brickfields, which supplied bricks for the expansion of the settlement. He was also a shareholder in the Suburban Hotel Company which built the gargantuan **Vale of Health Hotel** in 1863 to cater for the hordes of visitors to the Heath brought thither by the railway.

The Vale of Health c.1905, showing the hotel and the fairground run by the Gray family.

The immense Vale of Health Hotel, opened in 1863 as the Suburban Hotel, complete with tower and battlements. It was reduced by one floor later (see illustration on previous page).

After the Heath was purchased by the Metropolitan Board of Works in 1872, the Vale of Health could only expand within its existing confines, and by 1890 53 houses were crammed into the site. Despite the so-called vulgarity of its tavern, tea gardens and weekly funfair, held until the 1960s, it continued in the 20th century to attract distinguished inhabitants, such as Rabindranath Tagore (1861-1941), the Indian poet and mystic who lived briefly in 1912 at No.3 Villas-on-the-Heath; the writer D H Lawrence (1885--1930) and his wife Frieda at No.1 Byron Villas; and the painter Stanley Spencer (1891-1959) in studios above the Vale of Health hotel. In the 1920s the thriller writer Edgar Wallace (1875-1932) lived at Vale Lodge and novelist Stella Gibbons (1902-89) at Vale Cottage and in the next decade Lady Lucy Duff Gordon

('Lucille') (1862-1935), the couturier who had pioneered the use of brassieres, lived at No.6 Villas-on-the–Heath. She and her husband survived the *Titanic* disaster but the press suggested they had bribed the men to row them away in the first lifeboat virtually empty to avoid being swamped by drowning passengers. Her reputation never recovered. Compton Mackenzie (1883-1972) bought Woodbine Cottage in 1937 and lived there off and on for six years. In the 1970s Faircroft was the home of theatre luminaries Trevor Nunn and Janet Suzman, and actor Alan Bates (1934-2003) lived for many years at Lavender Cottage. In the same decade the pianist Alfred Brendel (b. 1931) lived at North Villa.

Two blocks of flats, the Athenaeum and Spencer House, arose in 1958 and 1964 respectively. Vale of Health

residents formed the Vale of Health Society in 1973 to resist inappropriate development and marked its 25th anniversary by founding *Heath Hands*, the first volunteer corps dedicated to Hampstead Heath. A recent plan by Camden Council to demolish Garden House on the banks of the pond and replace it with a building four times the size was overturned at the Court of Appeal after a legal battle led by the **Heath and Hampstead Society**. The village-like atmosphere of the Vale has been maintained and today it is one of Hampstead's most sought-after enclaves.

Vale of Health Hotel

Hampstead Heath station opened in 1860 and to cater for the expected influx of visitors an immense hotel was built by the Suburban Hotel Company, on the site of the old parish poor houses in the **Vale of Health**. Opened in 1863 as the Suburban Hotel (and also called the Vale of Health tavern) it had towers and battlements and accommodation for 2,000. Complete with pub, tea-gardens, grottoes and bowling alleys, it was not liked by local residents; Howitt was very critical of its "Tower of Babel bulk" and objected to pubs on the Heath "where people resort ostensibly for fresh air, relaxation, and exercise".

As a speculative venture the hotel failed. It was sold in 1876 and let as flats, and from the late 1890s the upper rooms were described as studios in rate books. Soon after it became a hotel again on a smaller scale, called the Vale of Health Hotel, which hosted a weekly funfair. Above the hotel the studios continued in use. Henry Lamb (1883-1960) painted his portrait of Lytton Strachey there in 1912. Stanley Spencer (1891-1959) was here in the 1920s painting his *The Resurrection, Cookham*. Too large to go down the stairs, this huge mural could only be removed by taking out the studio windows and lowering the painting outside the hotel. The Vale of Health studios closed in 1939 but the hotel was in business until 1960 when it was shut down by Hampstead Council. It was demolished in 1964 to make way for flats named after Spencer.

A smaller hotel, the chapel-like Hampstead Heath hotel, opened alongside in 1869 but had failed by 1871 and became a factory. In 1877 it passed to Henry Braun, who opened it as the Athenaeum club, the members including many foreigners and political radicals. From 1882 to 1886 the upper half of the building was let to the **Salvation Army**. Yet another hotel was opened next to the Athenaeum in the late 1880s but it had closed by 1903 and was replaced by Byron Villas. The Athenaeum, which had become an Anglo-German club by 1908, closed at the start of the Great War. The building became a factory and after World War Two a stage-scenery store. It was pulled down in 1958 to make way for flats.

Vane House

Vane Close off Rosslyn Hill marks the site of Vane House, demolished in 1970. The large red-brick mansion is associated with the vacillating politician Sir Henry Vane (1613-62), who managed to offend Charles I, Cromwell and Charles II; the last had 'Sir Harry Weather-vane', as he was nicknamed, executed on a trumped-up charge of treason. It has been suggested that Vane in fact lived at a house slightly to the north called **Slyes**. Vane House was certainly the home from 1781-95 of Admiral Matthew Barton (1715-95), who lent his title to **Admiral's House** although he never lived there. He retired here after an exciting career, which included being shipwrecked naked on the Barbary coast and carried into slavery by the Moors.

For the last 100 years or so of its life, Vane House became the Royal Soldiers' Daughters' Home. The institution began in 1855 as the Crimean War ended, and after three years in Rosslyn House the girls were marched up the hill to Vane House, led by Prince Albert. The trustees rebuilt it, incorporating part of the 17th-century house. Originally intended for destitute war orphans, it later took the daughters of serving or retired soldiers, who left at sixteen, some being trained to become teachers. After World War Two the girls were sent to

Vane House off Rosslyn Hill. From The Gentleman's Magazine *May 1828. The house was demolished in 1970.*

local maintained schools, and its school building in Fitzjohn's Avenue was sold off to become, in 1954, Fitzjohns Primary school. The home itself continued until Vane House was pulled down.

Washing

In the early 16th century Hampstead was said to be chiefly inhabited by washer-women. The quantity and purity of the water encouraged the nobility and London citizens to send their washing here and Tudor monarchs sent the palace laundry for a superior wash to Hampstead. The Heath was often festooned with washing laid out to dry on the broom and gorse bushes and a skipper on the Thames once remarked that it looked as if the heights of Hampstead were capped with snow.

Laundry work gave rise to the early name of Holly Hill, Cloth Hill. Claims that it was the main occupation of the first inhabitants of the Vale of Health are exaggerated, but the Vale did have the largest numbers of laundry posts in Hampstead in 1839. Clothes continued to be dried on the Heath; a laundress at North End was advertising this as late as 1870.

By then twenty laundries were listed at Hampstead, larger establishments than those of the earlier washerwomen. Later laundry firms included, in the 1880s the Fleet Laundry in Fleet Road, the Belsize Park Laundry and the South Hampstead Sanitary Laundry. Probably the biggest was the Hampstead Model Steam Laundry, on the east side of Cressy Road which lasted until **World War One**.

Water Supply

Springs on the Heath and southern slopes of the parish provided a plentiful water supply and also formed the tributaries of several London rivers. Three rivers rise in Hampstead: the Westbourne, the Tyburn and the Hampstead arm of the Fleet. All are now 'lost' or more correctly flow underground.

Most large houses had their own well or pump. Until the advent of piped water, public supplies for the town consisted principally of a pond – several of which disappeared during the spread of building in the 19th century – or a well, fed by a spring. A parish pond existed at the east end of Flask Walk in 1762, while in 1783 the town pump stood at the north end of the then narrow part of High Street. Other districts had similar water supplies through conduits, pumps, or ponds, fed by springs, or could draw on tributaries of the Westbourne. Belsize was supplied by tributaries of the Tyburn, one in Shepherd's fields, where the public spring was conduited and known as **Shepherd's well**.

The Hampstead Water Company formed in 1693 used the **Hampstead Ponds** to supply piped water, but not to Hampstead. The main piped supplies arrived in the 19th century. Pipes from Camden Town were extended to the southernmost part of the parish in the 1830s and 1840s, and in 1853 the New River Company extended pipes from Highgate to the top of the town, with a reservoir built at Hampstead Grove in 1856. In 1866 the West Middlesex Water Company obtained powers to serve parts of Hampstead, building a reservoir near **Kidderpore Hall** and by the 1880s was supplying all the parish roughly west of Haverstock Hill and Fitzjohn's Avenue, while the New River Company served the remainder.

Hampstead pioneered the erection of drinking fountains in London thanks to Henry Sharpe, a merchant of Heath Street who was inspired by Liverpool's example. The first opened in April 1859 with water supplied by the New River Company. Notable examples are the Palmer Memorial Fountain in **College Crescent** and the attractive fountain in **Well Walk**, restored to working order in honour of local historian Christopher Wade.

Well Walk

Takes its name from the chalybeate spring, the waters of which were an attraction in the 18th century when Hampstead was a spa, whose first buildings lay along this street. The **Wells & Campden Trust** laid out Gainsborough Gardens on the southern side of Well Walk in 1883; as part of that development, the first Long Room was demolished, although Wellside, "good Queen Anne work", was not built on the site until 1892. This was then the home of the theologian and writer Edwin Abbott (1838-1926), who proposed the fourth dimension, and later of the economist Lord Balogh of Hampstead (1905-85). Opposite is a drinking fountain which records the Gainsboroughs' gift of the land in 1698.

Many famous people have lived in Well Walk. Marie Stopes (1880-1958), the pioneer of birth control, came to No.14

Well Walk c. 1905, showing the commemorative fountain.

in 1909. Her traumatic experiences in Well Walk gave rise to her best-selling book *Married Love*. No.13 was the home of Poet Laureate John Masefield (1878-1967) in 1914-16. The actress Fay Compton (1894-1978) lived at No.22 in the early 1930s when J B Priestley (1894-1984) had his first London home at No.27. No.26 was occupied by the Irons family, including in the 1970s and 1980s their film-star son Jeremy and his actress wife Sinead Cusack.

The huge and hugely elaborate No.50, originally Thwaitehead but now Klippan House *(see p. 31)*, was built by and for the architect Ewan Christian (1814-95) in 1881 when he was adviser to the Church Commissioners. Here George Gilbert Scott Jnr urinated on the doorstep after Christian turned down one of his designs. Another Church architect, Temple Moore (1856-1920), lived at No.46 from 1892 to 1920.

Among the first residents at No.40 were the Constable family. After the death of his wife, **Constable** retained his Hampstead house as an occasional residence. In 1912 Frieda von Richthofen dumped her two daughters at No.40 before eloping with D H Lawrence (1885-1930) and five years later the couple found refuge at No.32 after eviction from Cornwall as suspected spies. E V Knox (1881-1971), editor of *Punch*, lived at No.34 from 1922 to 1945.

Fay Compton, resident of Well Walk.

J B Priestley (right) in a garden with writer Hugh Walpole.

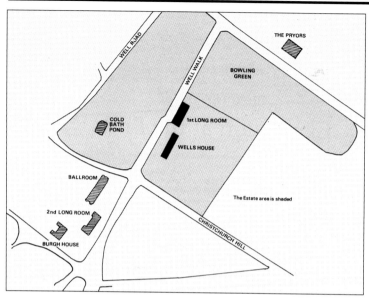

A plan showing the position of the first and second Long Rooms in Well Walk, with the location of the Cold Bath pond marked.

The site of the postman's house where Keats lodged with his dying brother Tom is now under the Wells Tavern. This pub replaced the Green Man in 1850, which itself replaced a 'tavern with Dancing Room', dating back to the Spa period. The tavern has always been owned by the **Wells & Campden Trust.**

The Wells

A well was publicized as early as 1653, when a popular broadsheet with a print of the **Hollow Tree** (*see p. 68*) by Wencelaus Hollar, praises Hampstead for its "Air, Hill, *Well* and School". Tokens of 1669 and 1670 that depict a well and bucket were inscribed 'the well in Hampstead', although that might refer to a shop near the village well rather than to the sale of medicinal waters. However, Celia Fiennes (1672-1741), likened the water from a Hampstead spring to that of Tunbridge Wells or Bath in

1697, the year before the grant of six swampy acres to the poor of Hampstead by the Gainsborough family, then Lords of the Manor. These acres included chalybeate (iron-rich) springs, whose medicinal qualities were already known.

The Wells Trust was formed and the water was being exploited by April 1700 when advertisements in the *Postman* stated that by direction of the trustees of the Wells it was carefully bottled up in flasks, and sent to Mr Phelps, Apothecary, at the Eagle and Child in Fleet Street every morning at the rate of 3d. per flask, and delivered for one penny more. In 1701 an entrepreneur, John Duffield, was found to take a 21-year lease of the land to develop it into a spa on the south side of Well Walk near the main well.

An 80-ft Great Room (or Long Room) was quickly built, which contained a small Pump Room to take the water, whose health giving qualities were endorsed by various doctors,

including William Gibbons of **Burgh House**. It also had a large Assembly Room where patients could recover and be entertained. Dancing, cards and concerts were organised, first advertised for the summer of 1701. All the latest popular pieces were included, duets by Purcell and songs from the current shows. The Great Room stood at the entrance to the present Gainsborough Gardens, which is on the site of the pleasure gardens. These had shaded walks and arbours and an ornamental pond; a bowling green was alongside. There soon arose a row of raffling (betting) shops, a tavern and a chapel (by 1716 doing a good trade in discreet or illicit marriages), all to the west.

Duffield's enterprise allowed the world of fashion to combine the quests for health and pleasure. So successful was he that in 1705, the year of Beau Nash's first visit to Bath, a comedy called *Hampstead Heath* was played at Drury Lane. London was shown as deserted in favour of Hampstead, where "the cards fly, the bowl runs, the dice rattle".

Unfortunately, Hampstead Wells became too popular with the wrong sort of Londoners. As early as 1709 there were complaints about swindlers and prostitutes and local residents were taking out lawsuits against riotous assemblies. John Macky warned in 1714 that its "nearness to London brings so many loose women in vampt-up old cloathes that modest company are ashamed to appear here". A decline set in, not helped by highway robberies and the sudden rise to popularity of Belsize. The end of the first and most

The first Long Room in Well Walk; watercolour by J P Emslie 1879. A view looking west.

colourful period in the history of the Wells came with the somewhat surprising conversion of the Great Room into a chapel of ease to the parish church in 1725, used as such until 1852 when **Christ Church** was opened. Later used as the drill hall for the **Hampstead Volunteers**, it was finally demolished in 1882.

After litigation the trustees were reconstituted in 1729 and attempted to revive the spa. The pump room was now in a small building below the Wells Tavern. Despite an eloquent treatise on the efficacy of the water from the local doctor, John Soame, less interest was shown in the waters than in a second Long Room and a Ball Room that were built near Burgh House in the 1730s. Hampstead thereafter prospered as a sedate middle-class resort rather than as a fashionable spa. Nevertheless

Pope, Johnson and Mrs Thrale were among the distinguished visitors, as well as Fanny Burney, whose heroine in *Evelina* wrote about the horrors of an evening at Hampstead Wells.

In the later part of the 18th century the spa buildings were used less for pleasure and more for community uses such as a courthouse and committee rooms, although the Long Room remained licensed for public entertainments until 1802. Then the second spa buildings were turned into residences. They were badly bombed in **World War Two** and, despite much protest, demolished in 1948. The Council built the flats called Wells House on the site. The waters had fallen into disuse by the mid 19th century.

The Wells & Campden Trust

In 1698 The Hon. Susannah Noel, on behalf of her son Baptist, Earl of Gainsborough, Lord of the Manor and a minor, granted six acres of Hampstead Heath to fourteen trustees, who were admitted as copyholders at a rent of 5s. a year, to use the income for the "sole use, benefit and advantage of the poor of the Parish of Hampstead for ever". The trustees leased all the property, except the spring-head north-west of the mineral spring, to John Duffield in 1701 for 21 years at £50 a year, on condition he spent £300 over three years improving it. The Trustees failed to collect any rent from the proprietors for the first 30 years, so there was initially no benefit to poor.

In 1729 a Chancery decree established the Wells Trust: the

estate was to be held of the lord for 5s. a year and a reasonable fine; the lord was to appoint fourteen resident copyholders as trustees and to nominate others when the number fell to five. Under the decree, the springhead had to be auctioned; it was leased to the brewer John Vincent and thereafter used only to supply the **Hampstead Brewery** in High Street and a few adjoining houses.

John Duffield sold his interest in 1730 to John Mitchell, who was granted leases for the remaining 42 years. In the same year the Trust paid £150 for repairing and fitting up the **Workhouse** in Frognal.

The earliest surviving minute book dates from 1783, when the charity had not met for seven years. But its estate was growing and it was able to disburse more to the poor, or in the parlance of the time 'decayed persons'. The Trust also paid for apprenticeships.

In 1876 the Trust built a block of model dwellings in Crockett's Court, called Wells Buildings, now Wells Court and were thereafter heavily involved in the Town Improvements (*see* **Slums**).

In 1880 the Wells charity was amalgamated with that set up by Elizabeth Hicks, Lady Campden, who in her will dated 1643 had bequeathed £200 to buy freehold land worth £10 a year, half of which was to relieve the most needy of Hampstead and half to apprentice boys. The twenty new trustees bought property in Flask Walk and Palmerston Road for baths and wash-houses (both sold to the Council in 1908), and in 1886 they bought land in Holly Bush Vale for artisans' dwellings,

The Wells Trust buildings in Oriel Place decorated for George V's coronation in 1910.

Campden Buildings. The Trust's income was spent on pensions, hospitals and dispensaries, and education.

In 1971 the trust was given a slightly different title, the Hampstead Wells and Campden Trust, having taken over several more recent charities with similar objectives, brought together in three funds: the Hampstead Relief in Sickness fund, the Hampstead Relief in Need fund, and the Wells & Campden Educational Foundation. In 2005 the Trust's administration was further streamlined by a Charity Commissioners' scheme.

The Trust today has assets of some £12 million and makes about 1,500 annual grants to individuals and organisations totalling £300,000. In addition, 150 elderly people receive pensions from the Trust.

West End

The core of West Hampstead, West End now seems further away from the parish church than either South End or North End, although it is closer. It was originally called le Rudyng, which indicates a woodland clearing, acquiring its present name by 1534. The hamlet was part of an estate belonging to Kilburn Priory and was later called Thorplands after the Thorpe family. There was a house on the estate by 1646 which may have been there four hundred years earlier.

By the Civil War period there were a number of houses and soon after London merchants built larger ones in what was an attractive retreat. However, before 1800 there were only about forty houses, lining the Green as far south as **West End House**. A proposal to bring Finchley Road to West End Lane in 1824 failed and the new road, laid out to the east, had little immediate effect. In 1851 West End was still a hamlet, mainly of agricultural labourers and tradespeople, with a handful of gentry. Its seclusion was destroyed just a few years later by the coming of the railways, with three lines crossing West End Lane. West End was to be transformed into **West Hampstead**.

The village was effectively destroyed at the end of the 19th century. Among the older buildings pulled down was the Cock and Hoop pub in 1900. Its alleged notoriety in its latter days was without foundation. Local temperance workers led a campaign of innuendo after the adjacent site was purchased in 1895 for a new parish church. Alexandra Mansions was built over the demolished pub.

West End Green

The old centre of West End, lined from the 17th century by large houses and to the north by its only tavern, the Cock and Hoop. A three-day fair was held annually on the Green until 1820, but was closed down after the event began to attract gangs of thieves who violently assaulted visitors. The Green once had a pond, fed by a stream that now leads underground into the Kilburn, but it was filled in as a danger to health in the mid 19th century. In 1875 the Green was granted by the Lord of the Manor to the builder John Culverhouse, who erected hoardings on it. These were torn down repeatedly by locals until the Vestry 'saved' the Green as a public open space by purchasing it in 1885.

West End Hall

Richard Gibbs, a goldsmith, acquired Hillfield on the east side of West End Lane in 1644, a house "new fronted and much beautified" after 1703 by Henry Binfield. This substantial property together with **West End House** dominated the village. It was home for most of the 19th century of the bookseller John Miles and his widow who died there in 1889 aged 98; she gave large haymaking parties in the 12-acre grounds and had persuaded the Vestry in 1844 to open a school for West End children. The last occupant of West End Hall was Major-General Sir C Crauford Fraser, who entertained the Prince of Wales at the house. The year following his death in 1896, the estate was sold for development. The house was roughly on the site of Nos.208-268 West End Lane.

West End House

West End House was the largest of the large houses in West End village. The 1762 estate map shows a substantial brick messuage, which was purchased in 1775 for Maria Beckford, mother of the Gothic novelist William who built the fantastical Fonthill Abbey. Eleven years later a large increase in rateable value suggests the house was rebuilt, and here Maria brought up William's two daughters, after his alleged involvement in a homosexual scandal, and the early death of his wife. The husband of one of the daughters, General Orde, later entertained the young Queen Victoria at the house. Daniel Whittle Harvey, who founded the *Sunday Times*, lived here until 1857. In that year the Hampstead Junction Railway was constructed along its

West End Green looking south, c. 1905.

southern boundary, and the house became a girls' Laundry Training School. By 1868 the northern boundary of the estate, sold to the British Land Company, was enclosed by the line of the Midland Railway who demolished the house itself in about 1871. Heysham Terrace was later built on the site.

West End Lane

A twisting route from Kilburn to Hampstead, lined largely by Victorian buildings. In its southern reaches it runs through land owned by the Powell-Cotton family who gave the streets they developed names derived from their estates in Kent – hence for example, Quex Road after their house in Birchington, and Acol Road. In the latter the Acol Bridge Club was based in the 1930s before their move to No.86 West End Lane. Its members originated the system of bidding which still bears the name of Acol.

Sydney Boyd Court is a council block named after an eminent surgeon who became mayor of Hampstead and covers the site of Anglebay, home of the architect Banister Fletcher (1833-99). No.167 was in the 1980s home to the composer Oliver Knussen. Behind Nos.99-145 were until 1882 the five-acre grounds of Oaklands Hall, built in 1826 and owned by a succession of well-known London shop-keepers, including the barber Francis Truefitt, the jeweller Charles Asprey and the outfitter, David Nicoll.

West Hampstead

In historical terms a relatively modern development which followed the construction of three railway lines south of the old village of West End. Large sections of several estates were sold to the railway companies, who required many acres of land for sidings and the like. The remaining farm- and parkland was cut into segments, which determined the street pattern. West End House was encircled by the Hampstead Junction Railway, built by 1857, and the Midland line, opened in 1868, and its estate was sold to the British Land Company, which constructed Iverson Road, and developed the land to the west, in Kilburn.

The period of greatest development was in the fifteen years from 1879, beginning with the opening of the third railway, the Metropolitan, with a station in West End Lane (West Hampstead). Donald Nicoll MP, a director of the railway company, in anticipation of its plans, laid out a road for which he received substantial com-pensation. He then sold his 23-acre estate, which he called West End Park, to the London Permanent Building Society, which was connected with Alexander Sherriff, a fellow MP and railway director, who gave his name to the northernmost road on the estate. Terraced houses were built in West End Park from 1879.

During the 1880s local builders developed the land north of the railway lines, with Dennington Park Road constructed on the line of an old path called Sweetbriar Walk. Land companies were involved in the spread of

housing on the Flitcroft estate near Fortune Green cemetery, whose presence ensured the new houses were aimed only at the lower middle-class – artisans, clerks and railway men – as in much of West Hampstead.

These estates were small and fragmented compared to those on the east of West End Lane, This area remained unchanged until the late 1890s when the three large houses there came on to the market. These were **West End Hall**; 18th-century Treherne House built over ancient Treherne Croft; and Canterbury House built on the ancient Jacksfield in the 1860s. Lymington and neighbouring roads were laid out about 1897. By 1913 building, mostly fair-sized semi-detached houses, was complete.

West Hampstead suffered during the Second World War, no doubt because of the railways, but large-scale rebuilding was avoided. As in many areas the main post-war trend was towards the refurbishing and conversion of old houses to flats, with young, single people replacing families. The widening of Finchley Road in the 1960s created a great traffic barrier divide between the heights of Hampstead and West Hamp-stead, which has quite a different feel to the village on the hill.

West Heath Road

Winding from Whitestone Pond down towards the Finchley Road, this follows a very old track from Hampstead town to **Child's Hill**. West Heath itself bears traces of Stone Age dwellings: a Mesolithic camp site of nomadic farmers of around

Whitestone Pond – a popular place in the days of horse-drawn traffic.

7,000 BCE and a Neolithic farming settlement in a forest clearing.

Just to the north of its junction with Branch Hill, an area much redeveloped in the 1980s, was The Grange, once the home of flamboyant actor-manager Sir Herbert Beerbohm Tree (1852-1917). He abandoned it in 1891 because of the problems of getting transport to "such a remote country spot".

The development of West Heath Road and the area to the south was delayed. A sewer had been laid down West Heath Road as early as 1884 and a skeletal road system including Redington Road and Heath Drive laid out, but it was only in the Edwardian period after 1900 that this district took on its modern shape.

The fields were quickly covered in an explosion of building to create Templewood Avenue and other new roads. The houses were intended for wealthy customers but without the formality of mid-Victorian houses. The developer George Hart working with the architect C H B Quennell built over 100 properties in this area. There were no shops and also no stabling: carriage-owning was no longer a requisite of high social standing.

The houses that face the Heath along West Heath Road are very large. Among them is the "unashamedly Hollywood Tudor" Sarum Chase, built in 1932 for artist Frank Salisbury (1874-1962) (hence 'Sarum') by his nephew Vyvyan. It was much frequented by royalty and politicians for portrait sittings. It has since been much used by film companies.

Whitestone Pond

One of Hampstead's best-known landmarks, this pond is situated at the highest point in North London, 440 ft above sea level and offers splendid views. It takes its name from a white milestone, whose sides were inscribed '4½ miles from Holborn bars' and 'IV miles from Giles Pound' and which once stood in the middle of the road. This now lies to the side among the bushes that were originally planted to discourage the **donkey** touts of Victorian times. Here they had their stands and offered rides; George du Maurier nicknamed Whitestone Pond 'Ponds Asinorum'.

Ramps at either end of the pond show that horse-drawn vehicles used to drive right through the pond *(see above)*, then known as Horse Pond, since it offered refreshment for the animals that had toiled up the hill. It began as a small dew pond but was enlarged and lined by the Vestry and by 1890 was artificially supplied with water. For many years, children used to paddle here and sail their boats, but the area is now a dangerous, polluted traffic complex.

To the east on the Heath below the road a brick pinfold or cattle pound was erected in 1787, to replace one removed from *Littleworth*. On the West Heath side of the pond, a flagstaff (now made of fibreglass) marks the site of a beacon, put up by 1576 as part of an early warning system, one of a chain of signal fires that was operated effectively in 1588 when a Spanish invasion was threatened. The first flagstaff was erected by the Lord of the Manor about 1845 and flew his flag (the cross of St George) whenever a Manorial Court was being held. The Old Court House is the name of the house to the north, but there is no evidence of courts being held here. The house was built in the 1780s by the owner of Jack Straw's Castle, where manorial courts were in fact held every Whitsun and Christmas, and which in the 19th century became the Manor Estate Office.

Windmills

The hill of Hampstead was crowned with two windmills. They can be seen on Visscher's *View of London* published before 1632. One was almost certainly in Hampstead Grove, as the title deeds of New Grove House are said to refer to a windmill. Nos.15-19 Holly Hill were converted from an old farmhouse and traditionally this is associated with the granary of the other windmill. The windmills gave their name to nearby Windmill Hill (*see Holly Hill*).

A windmill stood opposite the junction of **Shoot-up Hill**

The windmill at the junction of Mill Lane and Shoot-up Hill, destroyed by fire in 1861.

and Mill Lane (earlier Windmill Hill Lane) and may have been more used than those up the steep hill of Hampstead. It lasted until 1861 when a gale blew the sails round so fast that friction caused them to burst into flames.

Witches

There were a number of accusations of witchcraft in early 17th-century Hampstead. In 1604 the widow Alice Bradley was charged with witchcraft on four counts, two involving people who had "wasted in the body". She was acquitted. A few years later the yeoman William Hunt and his wife Joan were not so lucky. They appeared before magistrate Sir William Waad in 1612 on various charges of

witchcraft, including murder, and again in 1614 and found not guilty both times, but Joan was then found guilty of killing a three-year-old boy, having "practised certain detestable, impious and devilish arts, called witchcrafts". She was sentenced to be hanged.

Workhouse

Local paupers were at first housed in 'poorhouses'. Hampstead had poorhouses in Pond Street from 1670 and two were built at **Littleworth**. In 1778 the Vestry permitted Francis Willes to remove the latter, because he wished to enlarge his grounds, and rebuild them in the recently-drained Vale of Health. Three houses for paupers were erected there by 1779. A similar

A Tudor mansion in Frognal used as Hampstead's first workhouse as from 1729.

request was made in 1813 by the purchaser of property next to the Pond Street cottages, and freehold brick cottages were built for the poor at the eastern end of Flask Walk. In 1856 all the parish houses were offered for sale.

These cottages were additional to the parish workhouse. Rents and weekly allowances were financed from the poor rate which was set at a high 1s 6d in the pound. By opening a workhouse which could take twenty or more inmates the Vestry aimed to reduce the poor rate and hopefully provide better conditions for the poor. In 1729 it rented a large Tudor mansion in Frognal that had most recently been let as apartments; The **Wells Trust** gave a grant for its repair in 1730. It was however still not in a good condition; four years later hop sacks were hung against the walls to absorb the rain. Patched up in 1758, by 1800 it was so decayed that a new board of guardians was set up to consider the whole question of the poor.

The board purchased a house at New End, enlarged it,

and opened it as the new workhouse, for many more than the 80 who could be accommodated in the old one. When it opened in July 1801 there were approximately 130 inmates, a number which fluctuated according to the season but rose to 174 in 1814. Meanwhile the old house at Frognal fell into ruin and was taken down about 1810.

In 1837 Hampstead was combined with six other parishes in Edmonton poor law union and from 1842 paupers were placed in a new workhouse at Edmonton. However, Hampstead successfully sought separation from the union because it was under-represented on the board and in 1848 became a poor law authority in its own right, with its own eleven-strong elected Board of Guardians. The new Board decided to replace the New End workhouse with a new purpose-built building, designed by H E Kendall. The new building not only provided accommodation for paupers but offices for the Vestry until the Vestry Hall opened on Haverstock Hill in 1878.

Jobs given to inmates were unpleasant. Corn-grinding and oakum-picking were common tasks. Men were put to breaking stones before breakfast was provided and it was said the fragments had to be small enough to pass through the iron grille on the workshop window. 'Abatement of diet' was just one of the harsh punishments for idleness.

A four-storey pavilion block infirmary was erected in 1870, including features such as sanitary towers projecting from the building, and tall windows (one for every two beds) at each side to provide cross-ventilation and sunlight. Growth in demand for hospital accommodation led to the erection of a further ward building in 1884-5. The infirmary's medical officer Dr Cook, proposed the construction of a circular tower ward, which had begun to appear on the continent. Designed by Charles Bell, it comprised three floors of wards, with nurses' accommodation on an attic floor, and a 12,000 gallon water tank at the top. The building cost £12,000 and is the earliest surviving example of its type in the country. It is now Listed. In 1905 a final main extension up to Heath Street was built.

During **World War One** Hampstead workhouse was used as a convalescent home for wounded soldiers. The hospital was taken over by the London County Council and used as a general hospital known as New End Hospital. The old workhouse was used as administrative offices and staff accommodation. The hospital closed in 1985 and the surviving buildings were then refurbished for residential use.

World War One

During the war large areas of the Heath were turned over to allotments and military watch-stations. Several volunteer corps used the Heath as a training ground. One such was the Artists' Rifles, otherwise known as the 28th Battalion of the London Regiment, converted into a territorial force under Lord Haldane's army reorganisation in 1907. When they marched up Fitzjohn's Avenue en route to the Heath, they were halted and young ladies would appear with food and drink. At the top of the Heath by Whitestone Pond a pale blue anti-aircraft gun was installed in 1916.

In July that year the Hampstead War Hospital Supply Depot opened at No.91 Finchley Road. Female voluntary labour was used to produce hospital supplies e.g.

bandages, splints, swabs and clothing for hospitals at home and abroad.

The wounded were put up in any available large house. Unfortunately, those available were often damp, draughty and without proper drainage. Cedar Lawn, for example, at North End Way was about to be pulled down when it was offered to Hampstead's Red Cross Voluntary Aid Department. Rosslyn Lodge became an Auxiliary Hospital, opened in summer 1916. The workhouse was used as a convalescent home for wounded soldiers.

Hampstead suffered three Zeppelin raids during the war, which caused slight damage. These were on 4 September 1917, 7 March 1918 and 19 May 1918, when bombs fell on Haverstock Hill. The last was also the last Zeppelin raid on London.

World War Two

Like many London boroughs Hampstead suffered bombing near the start and towards the end of the war. In 1940-41 330 houses were destroyed and over 10,500 damaged. In 1944 there were ten flying bomb incidents and by the autumn of that year over 13,700 houses had been damaged. V2 rocket attacks followed in early 1945. There were over 1,100 casualties, 200 of which were fatal. Hampstead town itself escaped the worst of the bombs, except in New End where in two acres bounded by Well Walk, New End Square, and Christchurch Hill, only five houses survived and the second **Wells** Long Room and ballroom were destroyed.

The worst hit area was West Hampstead, with its concentration of railway lines. Broadhurst Gardens was the

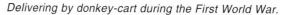

Delivering by donkey-cart during the First World War.

Destruction by V2 rocket at Hampstead Central Library, Arkwright Road in 1945.

most bomb damaged road in the borough. One of the last major incidents was when a V2 fell on Hampstead Central Library in Arkwright Road, which was being used as an ARP warden's post. A lady warden was killed but luckily there were only fourteen other casualties, despite 800 houses nearby suffering damage.

Much sand was extracted from the Heath to fill sandbags which were used to strengthen shelters, such as the one by the second Wells buildings. After an initial ban on using them tube stations were also used as shelters. Henry Moore made many sketches of those taking refuge at **Belsize Park tube station**. Sometimes social groups were set up. Regular shelterers at Swiss Cottage even produced their own bulletin and campaigned for better facilities – they objected to having to take a train to Finchley Road to find a proper toilet.

Warship Weeks were organised. Many places

adopted a particular vessel. Hampstead adopted *HMS Quilliam*, commissioned in 1942, which served in the Far East, and was later sold to the Dutch Navy and renamed. The office of the Flag Officer Submarines (FOS), one of the most important shore establishments of the Navy, was based in Hampstead from 1940 to 1944, in Northways block in Finchley Road by College Crescent. FOS Wrens were billeted in two villas in Broadhurst Gardens, but more space was needed and Charing Cross Nurses' Home in England's Lane was requisitioned in 1942 for the duration of the war.

Many Londoners were made homeless as a result of bombing. After the war, prefabricated houses, or 'prefabs', were erected in many boroughs to ease the housing shortage. The US government gave a number of prefabs to Hampstead which were erected close to the border with Hendon, in Westcroft Close

(named after a former farm in the neighbouring borough). Designed to last ten years they were eventually demolished in the 1980s and replaced by the council estate of the same name.

Wyldes

Perhaps the most picturesque place in North End, straddling the border of Hampstead and Hendon. The two houses, now called Old Wyldes and Wyldes, were respectively the farmhouse and barn of the 340-acre estate; the farmland has been absorbed by the Hampstead Heath Extension and Hampstead Garden Suburb. In medieval times, the estate was owned by the leper hospital of St James (where St James's Palace now stands), and for 370 years it belonged to Eton College. From c.1785 to 1854 the farm was let to the Collins family and took their name. In the 1820s the young artist, John Linnell (1792-1882), was lodging here with his family and was often visited by his future son-in-law, Samuel Palmer, and by the aged William Blake, whom Linnell had befriended. Linnell's 1831 painting of the farm depicts a pastoral idyll reminiscent of a Constable landscape. Dickens was another distinguished lodger here in 1837, when recovering from the death of his beloved sister-in-law, Mary Hogarth.

The farmers had gone by 1884, when Charlotte Wilson (1854-1944) lived here and started a revolutionary study circle called the Hampstead Historic Club. This was not concerned with local history, but with Fabian ideology, and Wyldes became a meeting place for Bernard Shaw, Sidney Webb, E Nesbit and other

Wyldes Farm, North End. Watercolour by George Barnard, 1830.

radical thinkers.

In 1906, the whole property was taken over by the Hampstead Garden Suburb Trust, partly as its estate office and partly as the home of its chief architect, Sir Raymond Unwin (1863-1940). A plaque notes his residence here 1906-40. It was badly damaged by fire in 1981 but has been restored.

X Y Z

To complete this A to Z compilation:

X is for xenophobia. After the *Lusitania* was sunk in May 1915 any shop with a German-sounding name was vulnerable to anti-German feeling. Although rioting was nowhere near as bad in Hampstead as in East London, a barber's in Fleet Road was wrecked.

Y is for Robert Yeo. This Devon-born speculative builder was busy on the **Eton Estate**, where Samuel Cuming was the primary developer early on. King Henry's Road, for example, was begun by Cuming in 1856 but continued by Yeo into the 1870s in what F M L Thompson called a "good deal more skimped and debased" style.

Z is for Anne Ziegler (1910-2003), one half of one of Britain's most popular singing acts during and after World War Two. Born Irene Frances Eastwood in Liverpool, she married tenor Webster Booth (1902-84) in 1938 and they toured Britain performing popular ballads such as *Only a Rose* and *We'll Gather Lilacs*. They lived at No.102 Frognal, an Edwardian cottage designed by Amyan Champneys, son of Basil.

As can be imagined this is merely a selection. The history of Hampstead is a rich mine for the local historian and the interested reader is urged to undertake their own research. Some suggested books are listed under Further Reading.

Further Reading

Baines, F E, *Records of the Manor, Parish and Borough of Hampstead* (1890).

Barratt, Thomas J, *Annals of Hampstead* (1912).

Bentwich, Helen, *The Vale of Health* (1968).

Camden History Reviews

Camden History Society, *Streets of Belsize* (2009).

Camden History Society, *The Streets of West Hampstead* (1992).

Cherry, Bridget & Pevsner, Nikolaus, *The buildings of England. London 4: North* (1998).

Clark, Leonard, *A Prospect of Hampstead and Highgate* (1967).

Colloms, Marianne and Windling, Dick, *The Greville Estate: the history of a Kilburn neighbourhood* (Camden History Society 2007)

Emerson, Ellen, Harman, Ruth and Thomson, Diana (eds.), *Hampstead Memories* (2000).

Farmer, Alan, *Hampstead Heath* (1984).

Gee, Christina, *Hampstead and Highgate in old photographs 1870-1918* (1974).

Hart, Valerie and Marshall, Lesley, *Wartime Camden* (1983).

Hill, Mary, *Hampstead in light and shade* (1938).

Holmes, Malcolm, *Hampstead to Primrose Hill* (1995).

Howitt, William, *The Northern Heights of London* (1869).

Jenkins, Simon and Ditchburn, Jonathan, *Images of Hampstead* (1982).

Maxwell, Anna, *Hampstead: its historic houses, its literary and artistic associations* (1912).

Mitton, G E, *Hampstead and Marylebone* (1902).

Norrie, Ian and Mavis (eds.), *The Book of Hampstead* (1968).

Oxford Dictionary of National Biography (on line).

Park, J J, *The topography and natural history of Hampstead* (1814).

Pevsner, Nikolaus, *The buildings of England — London II* (1952).

Richardson, John, *Hampstead One Thousand* (1985).

Service, Alastair, *Victorian and Edwardian Hampstead* (1989).

Smith, Clive and David, *Hampstead Past and Present* (2002).

Sullivan, David, *The Westminster Corridor: The Anglo-Saxon story of Westminster Abbey and its lands in Middlesex* (1994).

Thompson, F M L, *Hampstead, Building a Borough 1650-1954* (1974).

Tindall, Gillian, *Two Hundred Years of London Justice: The Story of Hampstead and Clerkenwell Magistrates Courts* (2001).

Usborne, Ann, *A Portrait of Hampstead* (1984).

Victoria History of the County of Middlesex, Vol. IX (1989).

Wade, Christopher, *For the Poor of Hampstead, for ever* (1998).

Wade, Christopher, *The Streets Of Hampstead* (Camden History Society 2000).

Wade, Christopher, *Hampstead Past* (1989).

Walford, Edward, *Old and New London, Vol. V* (c.1880).

White, Caroline, *Sweet Hampstead and its associations* (1900).